The History of
Terrorism

Other titles in the Lucent Terrorism Library are:

America Under Attack: Primary Sources
America Under Attack: September 11, 2001
Terrorists and Terrorist Groups

THE
LUCENT
TERRORISM
LIBRARY

The History of Terrorism

Robert Taylor

LUCENT BOOKS
SAN DIEGO, CALIFORNIA

THOMSON
™
GALE

Detroit • New York • San Diego • San Francisco
Boston • New Haven, Conn. • Waterville, Maine
London • Munich

Library of Congress Cataloging-in-Publication Data

Taylor, Robert.
  History of terrorism / by Robert Taylor.
    p.   cm. — (Terrorism library series)
Summary: Examines the political agendas, actions and religious beliefs of individuals and groups who,
throughout history, have resorted to violent actions in order to generate fear and gain their objectives.
Includes bibliographical references and index.
  ISBN 1-59018-206-5 (hardpack : alk. paper)
  1. Terrorism—History—Juvenile literature. 2. Terrorism—Religious aspects—Juvenile literature. 3.
Terrorism—Political aspects—Juvenile Literature. [1. Terrorism—History. 2. Terrorism—Religious
aspects. 3. Terrorism—Political aspects.] I. Title. II. Series.
  HV6431 .T426 2002
  303.6'25—dc21

2002001910

Contents

Foreword

It was the bloodiest day in American history since the battle of Antietam during the Civil War—a day in which everything about the nation would change forever. People, when speaking of the country, would henceforth specify "before September 11" or "after September 11." It was as if, on that Tuesday morning, the borders had suddenly shifted to include Canada and Mexico, or as if the official language of the United States had changed. The difference between "before" and "after" was that pronounced.

That Tuesday morning, September 11, 2001, was the day that Americans began to learn firsthand about terrorism, as first one fuel-heavy commercial airliner, and then a second, hit New York's World Trade Towers—sending them thundering to the ground in a firestorm of smoke and ash. A third airliner was flown into a wall of the Pentagon in Washington, D.C., and a fourth was apparently wrestled away from terrorists before it could be steered into another building. By the time the explosions and collapses had stopped and the fires had been extinguished, more than three thousand Americans had died.

Film clips and photographs showed the horror of that day. Trade Center workers could be seen leaping to their deaths from seventy, eighty, ninety floors up rather than endure the 1,000-degree temperatures within the towers. New Yorkers who had thought they were going to work, were caught on film desperately racing the other way to escape the wall of dust and debris that rolled down the streets of lower Manhattan. Photographs showed badly burned Pentagon secretaries and frustrated rescue workers. Later pictures would show huge fire engines buried under the rubble.

It was not the first time America had been the target of terrorists. The same World Trade Center had been targeted in 1993 by Islamic terrorists, but the results had been negligible. The worst of such acts on American soil came in 1995 at the hands of a home-grown terrorist whose hatred for the government led to the bombing of the federal building in Oklahoma City. The blast killed 168 people—19 of them children.

But the September 11 attacks were far different. It was terror on a frighteningly well-planned, larger scale, carried out by nineteen men from the Middle East whose hatred of the United States drove them to the most appalling suicide mission the world had ever witnessed. As one U.S. intelligence officer told a CNN reporter, "These guys turned airplanes into weapons of mass destruction, landmarks familiar to all of us into mass graves."

Some observers say that September 11 may always be remembered as the date that the people of the United States finally came face to face with terrorism. "You've been relatively sheltered from terrorism," says an Israeli terrorism expert. "You hear about it happening here in the Middle East, in Northern Ireland, places far away from you. Now Americans have joined the real world where this ugliness is almost a daily occurrence."

This "real world" presents a formidable challenge to the United States and other nations. It is a world in which there are no rules, where modern terrorism is war not waged on soldiers, but on innocent people – including children. Terrorism is meant to shatter people's hope, to create instability in their daily lives, to make them feel vulnerable and frightened. People who continue to feel unsafe will demand that their leaders make concessions—*do something*—so that terrorists will stop the attacks.

Many experts feel that terrorism against the United States is just beginning. "The tragedy is that other groups, having seen [the success of the September 11 attacks] will think: why not do something else?" says Richard Murphy, former ambassador to Syria and Saudi Arabia. "This is the beginning of their war. There is a mentality at work here that the West is not prepared to understand."

Because terrorism is abhorrent to the vast majority of the nations on the planet, President George W. Bush's declaration of war against terrorism was supported by many other world leaders. He reminded citizens that it would be a long war, and one not easily won. However, as many agree, there is no choice; if terrorism is allowed to continue unchecked the world will never be safe.

The four volumes of the Lucent Terrorism Library help to explain the unexplainable events of September 11, 2001 as well as examine the history and personalities connected with terrorism in the United States and elsewhere in the world. Annotated bibliographies provide readers with ideas for further research. Fully documented primary and secondary source quotations enliven the text. Each book in this series provides students with a wealth of information as well as launching points for further study and discussion.

Introduction

Defining Terrorism

Terrorism has appeared in history wearing many disguises. It has been used by revolutionaries to correct what they perceived as political and economic injustice; by rebels seeking to throw off what they claimed to be the exploitative yoke of colonial oppression; by ethnic and religious minorities fighting to secede from communities they believed were persecuting them. It has been used by advocates of both radical and conservative political agendas; by workers and management in labor disputes; and by those whose only goal was to inflict pain and suffering on members of races and other social groups that they imagined posed a threat to their way of life. Finally, it has been used by governments as an instrument of repression to paralyze opposition.

The tactics of terrorism are always violent. Over the centuries, terrorists have employed daggers, guns, and bombs to kill and destroy; they have also staged kidnappings and hijackings to intimidate and coerce. Technological advances threaten to make the terrorists' arsenal even more deadly and frightening. On September 11, 2001, terrorists transformed jet airplanes into weapons of mass destruction, killing thousands in attacks on the World Trade Center in New York and the Pentagon in Washington, D.C. There is even evidence that terrorist groups have access to chemical and biological agents and perhaps nuclear devices.

The diversity of aims and methods that have characterized terrorism has created a problem for students of the subject. Experts have had difficulty defining exactly what terrorism is. In his book, *Encyclopedia of Terrorism and Political Violence*, historian and political scientist John Richard Thackrah lists sixty-seven different definitions; few of these definitions fully agree with each other and many are, at least in part, contradictory. Another source of confusion that plagues many discussions of terrorism is the nature of the word itself. To call an event an act of terrorism, in most contexts, expresses a negative value judgment about it. Terrorists rarely apply the term to themselves, preferring instead descriptions like "freedom fighter" or "revolutionary." Yasir Arafat, the head of the Palestine Liberation Organization who has been widely accused by the governments of Israel and the United States of masterminding hundreds of terrorist attacks, illustrated this dilemma when he addressed the United Nations in 1974. "The difference between a revolutionary and a terrorist lies in the reason for which each fights," Arafat said. "For whoever stands by a just cause and fights for the freedom and liberation of his land from invaders ... cannot possibly be called a terrorist."[1]

The phrase "one man's terrorist is another man's freedom fighter" occurs frequently in studies of political violence. Bias inevitably creeps into the discussion because it is difficult to be neutral on such a fundamental ethical issue as the circumstances—if indeed there are any—that justify putting human life at risk. "What is called terrorism thus seems to depend on one's point of view," explains political scientist Brian Jenkins.

Use of the term implies a moral judgment; and if one party can successfully attach the label "terrorist" to its opponent, then it has indirectly persuaded others of its moral viewpoint. Hence, the decision to call someone or label

some organization "terrorist" becomes almost unavoidably subjective, depending largely on whether one sympathizes with or opposes the person/group/cause concerned. If one identifies with the victim of the violence, for example, then the act is terrorism. If, however, one identifies with the perpetrator, the violent act is regarded in a more sympathetic, if not positive ... light; and it is not terrorism.[2]

Smoke billows from the twin towers of the World Trade Center following the violent attacks of September 11, 2001.

Definitions of Terrorism

Scholars have offered numerous definitions of terrorism. The following, from Encyclopedia of Terrorism and Political Violence, *by John Richard Thackrah, are eight of the most useful attempts to sum up in a few words this complex and controversial phenomenon.*

"Sociologically, terror is a . . . practice that causes intense fear or suffering, whose aim is to intimidate, subjugate, especially as a political weapon or policy. Politically, its main function is to intimidate and disorganize the government through fear, [so that] through this political changes can be achieved."—J. S. Roucek

"An action of violence is labeled terrorist when its psychological effects are out of proportion to its purely physical result."—R. Aron

"Political terrorism can be defined as a strategy, a method by which an organized group or party tries to get attention for its aims, or force concessions toward its goals, through the systematic use of deliberate violence."—F. M. Watson

"Political terrorism is a special form of clandestine, undeclared and unconventional warfare waged without humanitarian restraints or rules."—P. Wilkinson

"Terrorism can be used to create an atmosphere of despair or fear, to shake the faith of ordinary citizens in their government and its representatives."—B. M. Leiser

"[Terrorism is characterized by] a series of individual acts of extraordinary and intolerable violence, a constant pattern of symbolic or representative selection [of targets], and is deliberately intended to create a psychological effect on specific groups of people."—M. Crenshaw

"Terrorism may be defined as systematic and organized violence against non-resisting persons to create fear in them for the purpose of retaining or gaining governmental authority."—M. Karanovic

"Terrorism is the use or threat of extraordinary political violence to induce fear, anxiety or alarm in a target audience wider than the immediate symbolic victims. Terrorism is violence for political effect as opposed to military impact."—E. S. Heyman

---

Despite these difficulties, most definitions share a number of characteristics that help distinguish terrorism from other forms of politically motivated violence.

First, terrorism, as its name implies, makes use of violence not just to destroy property or take life but also to inspire terror in people other than its primary victims. It is for this reason that terrorists often target innocent members of a population. Perpetrators of terrorist acts wish to generate fear that no one is safe, undermining people's faith in their government's ability to protect citizens as they go about their daily lives and thus create an atmosphere of insecurity and instability.

Second, terrorism is a tactic usually employed by people who feel they do not have enough power to challenge those whom they perceive to be their enemy more directly (for example, by a mass uprising).

Third, unlike guerrilla warriors, terrorists do not seek to conquer and hold territory. As a rule, terrorists feel they do not have enough resources (manpower and weaponry) to conduct a full-fledged military campaign. They content themselves with sporadic acts, hoping to inspire more extensive forms of political violence at a later date.

Fourth, unlike guerrilla armies, which have a centralized command structure, terrorist organizations are usually decentralized. Although there is often a leader who sets general goals, specific operations are carried out by small groups, called cells, which act autonomously. Furthermore, to preserve security, the members of one cell may not even know the identities of the members of other cells.

Fifth, terrorism needs publicity to survive. To achieve the goal of generating widespread anxiety and instability, the details of an act of terrorism must be broadcast to the greatest number of people. For that reason, terrorists frequently choose targets that have symbolic significance to guarantee maximum media coverage.

Finally, there are two common myths about terrorism that must be dispelled before an undistorted view of the subject can emerge. The first is that terrorists are irrational. Despite newspaper headlines which refer to them as "madmen," terrorists who have been arrested and subjected to psychological examination have tended to score within the normal range on standard personality tests. Terrorists are also not given to random acts of violence; they are coldly deliberate in their choice of victims and they carefully calculate their acts to win the maximum amount of publicity for their cause.

The second myth is that terrorism is a recent phenomenon. In fact, as its history will reveal, terrorism has been a factor in disputes between human beings for thousands of years. The motives for terrorism have changed very little over the centuries: political, economic, religious, and ethnic differences that have proved immune to peaceful solution. What has changed dramatically is the destructive power of the weapons terrorists have at their disposal. Daggers, the weapon of choice among early terrorists, can kill one person at a time. Technology has now put weapons of mass destruction into the hands of otherwise powerless groups of dissidents. A single act of terrorism can now claim thousands of lives, making a dispassionate understanding of why some people resort to its methods more important than ever.

Chapter One

Zealots, Assassins, and the Reign of Terror

Terrorism began in the first century A.D. Prior to that time, political violence took the form of wars between rival kingdoms, empires, or cities; campaigns of conquest, as when Alexander the Great set out to subdue the known world; and revolts and other mass uprisings. Political assassination was another prevalent phenomenon in the ancient world, and it has been described as a precursor of terrorism. But there is an important distinction. When a king, emperor, or other leader was killed, it was usually by a rival who sought merely to replace him, leaving the basic political, social, and economic structures of the realm unchanged. Terrorism, by contrast, seeks more fundamental changes in the way a society is organized. For example, the Zealots, history's first terrorists, aimed to transform first-century Judea from a province of the Roman Empire into a theocratic Jewish state.

The Zealots

In the year 63 B.C., Roman legions commanded by the general Pompey overran Judea and turned the Jewish homeland into a client kingdom of the Roman Empire. Some fifty years later, the emperor Augustus completed the domination when he deposed the local political leadership and installed a Roman governor. Thereafter, the Jews had to pay onerous taxes to their conquerors, driving many of them into debt. Equally distressing, the taxes had to be paid in the currency of the empire, which bore the image of the emperor, whom the Romans regarded as a god. This was very offensive to the Jews, whose monotheistic religion forbade them from recognizing any deity other than their own.

Resistance to the Roman occupation flared into violence from time to time. The most notable of these episodes was an uprising led by a man called Judas of Gamala. The Roman army, vastly superior in numbers, quickly defeated the rebels, but the revolt left two important legacies. First, it fostered the idea among many Jews that it was legitimate to take up arms in defense of their territory and their beliefs. Second, the Jewish authorities, led by the high priest of the Temple in Jerusalem, opposed the revolt, advocating a policy of accommodation with the Romans. Their stance split Jewish society between those who were prepared to accept Roman rule in exchange for favored status and those who utterly opposed the foreign occupiers. The division occurred along class lines, the wealthy siding with the Romans and the impoverished peasantry eager to continue the armed struggle. Furthermore, many Jews considered the behavior of the upper class to be sacrilegious.

This inflammatory situation became a crisis in A.D. 66. The Roman emperor Nero needed money to finance his extravagant life. Since taxes were already as high as the Judean population could bear, Nero confiscated gold and other treasures from the Temple vault. The Jews protested, and many were arrested and crucified. Yet the high priest Ananus, along with many others among the priesthood and the upper class, continued to urge collaboration with the Romans, fearing that

Roman soldiers advance toward a smoky Jerusalem, driving the Zealots out of the city. The Romans defeated the Zealots in A.D. 74.

open revolt would be met with harsh repression. Tension mounted and eventually exploded when a rebel named Menahem raided the Roman mountaintop garrison at Masada, outside of Jerusalem, seized many weapons, and killed hundreds of occupying soldiers.

Menahem convinced his followers, who called themselves Zealots because of their unwavering devotion to their conception of Jewish law, that he was the messiah, whose divinely appointed role was to establish the kingdom of God on Earth. Under Menahem's leadership, the Zealots drove the Romans out of Jerusalem and launched a campaign of terror and assassination against the invaders' Jewish collaborators. The violence was conducted primarily by an ultra-extremist element called Sicarii (a Greek word meaning "dagger bearers") because their weapon of choice was a small but lethal knife they concealed in the folds of their robes. The Sicarii

spread the rumor that the bloodshed was a divine punishment occasioned by those who had strayed from Jewish law by casting their lot with the Romans, and they claimed that no one would be safe from the wrath of God until all the people joined with them to rid Judea of the pagan presence.

The Effects of Zealot Terror

The principal source of information about the Zealots and Sicarii is Josephus, a first-century Jewish historian who had been educated in both Jewish and Roman schools and was a member of one of the ruling families of Judea. Josephus opposed the Roman occupation, but he was also shocked by the terrorism that claimed the lives of many of his friends and associates. Caught in the middle of the dispute between the rebels and the collaborators, he provides a unique perspective on the events that engulfed his world. In a book called *History of the Jewish War*, Josephus

A Justification for Political Assassination

The Roman philosopher Cicero was opposed to violence, but in his work De Officiis *(quoted in* The Terrorism Reader, *edited by Walter Laqueur and Yonah Alexander), he makes an important exception in the case of tyrants. Terrorists have used similar arguments to justify their actions ever since.*

"There is no greater crime than to murder a fellow man, especially a friend. Still who would say that he commits a crime who assassinates a tyrant, however close a friend?

The people of Rome, I tell you, think it no crime, but the noblest of all noble deeds.... It is not repugnant to nature to despoil [ruin], if you can, those whom it is a virtue to kill; nay this pestilent and godless brood should be utterly banished from human society. For as we amputate a limb in which the blood and the vital spirit have ceased to circulate, because it injures the rest of the body, so monsters, who, under human guise, conceal the cruelty and ferocity of a wild beast, should be severed from the common body of humanity."

describes the Sicarii's tactics and the terror they inspired:

> There sprang up another sort of robbers in Jerusalem, which were called Sicarii, who slew men in the day time, and in the midst of the city; this they did chiefly at the festivals, when they mingled themselves among the multitude, and concealed daggers under their garments, with which they stabbed those that were their enemies; and when any fell down dead, the murderers became part of those that had indignation against them; by which means they appeared persons of such reputation that they could by no means be discovered. The first man who was slain by them was Jonathan, a priest, after whose death many were slain every day, while the fear men were in of being so served was more afflicting than the calamity itself; and while every body expected death every hour, as men do in war, so men were obliged to look before them, and to take notice of their enemies at a great distance; nor, if their friends were coming to them, durst [dare] they trust them any longer.[3]

Elsewhere in *History of the Jewish War*, Josephus reports that success in their campaign of terror caused the Sicarii to grow bolder, and they raided and burned villages outside of Jerusalem. In one such attack, he says, they massacred seven hundred people, including many women, children, and elderly. The terrorists increased the panic they had

Flavius Josephus documented the violence and bloodshed of the Zealots' terrorist tactics.

created by carrying out acts of violence in the Temple itself, convincing many devout Jews that the defilement of such a holy place would bring the wrath of God upon the community. According to Josephus, the high priest Ananus declared death would have been preferable to witnessing the desecration: "Certainly it had been good for me to die before I had seen the house of God full of so many abominations, or these sacred places, that ought not to be trodden upon at random, filled with the feet of these blood-shedding villains."[4]

Shortly afterward, the Sicarii apprehended Ananus and murdered him on the

Temple steps in front of the eyes of hundreds of horrified onlookers. In addition to assassination, the Sicarii also employed two tactics that have come to be associated with more modern versions of terrorism. They took hostages and used them to ransom their own members who had been arrested by the authorities. They also held mock trials of captured dignitaries to publicize their cause. "They had the impudence of setting up fictitious tribunals and judicatures [courts] for that purpose," Jospehus writes. "As they intended to have Zacharias the son of Baruch, one of the most eminent of the citizens, slain, so…they called together, by public proclamation, 70 men of the populace, for a show, as if they were real judges, while they had no proper authority."[5]

The End of the Zealots

The violence of the Zealots and the Sicarii eventually reached such a pitch that Jerusalem was paralyzed with fear. Josephus claims that many among the population were unable to endure the climate of terror:

> They were so scourged and [psychologically] tortured, that their bodies were not able to sustain their torments, till at length and with difficulty, they had the favor to be slain. The terror that was upon the people was so great, that no one had the courage enough either to weep openly for the dead man that was related to them, or to bury him; but those that were shut up in their own houses could only shed tears in secret, and durst not even groan without great

caution, lest any of their enemies should hear them; for if they did, those that mourned for others soon underwent the same death with those whom they mourned for.[6]

The terrorism had weakened Jerusalem so much that the Roman army had little difficulty in driving the Zealots from the city and burning the Temple to the ground. For several years, the remnants of the group staged skirmishes in the countryside, but they were eventually forced to take refuge at Masada in A.D. 74. Surrounded by Roman legions, the remaining terrorists, some 960 in number and led by a man called Eleazar ben Yar, elected to commit mass suicide rather than be captured.

When the Romans marched into the mountain fortress, they expected to meet with resistance. Instead, says historian Bruce Scott,

> An eerie silence greeted them. Buildings were on fire. Smoke wafted through the early morning light. But no enemy confronted them…. Two women and five children appeared. From them, Silva [the Roman commander] learned the truth. During the night, Eleazar ben Yar had made an impassioned speech to his beleaguered compatriots. "Let us die before we become slaves under our enemies," he had said, "and let us go out of this world, together with our children and our wives, in a state of freedom." Stirred to their souls, the assembled agreed to a mass suicide

pact. Fathers tearfully dispatched their wives and children. The rest were killed by 10 men chosen by lot. Of those 10, one was chosen by lot to kill the other nine. Upon setting fire to the various complexes, the remaining Zealot took his own life. The surviving women and children had hidden themselves in the underground caverns to escape the terror.[7]

The Zealots exhibited a number of features that have become part of the standard profile of more modern terrorist groups. Their motives were both political and religious. Indeed, most historians agree that they did not distinguish between the realms of politics and religion at all, much in the same way that contemporary Islamic terrorists are attempting to achieve fundamentally religious objectives through political means. The Zealots' terrorist branch, the Sicarii, operated in secret and in a way that was guaranteed to generate maximum publicity and engender the greatest amount of fear among the people of Judea. They were also uncompromising: Even though their tactics were self-defeating, making it

960 Zealots committed mass suicide at the Fortress of Masada (pictured).

The Zealots committed mass suicide rather than live under Roman rule.

easier for the Romans to subjugate the land the Zealots claimed to be trying to free from domination, they refused to swerve from the violent course they had set for themselves.

The Assassins

The Assassins were another premodern terrorist group. Like the Zealots, they were motivated by a blend of political and religious factors, and they were equally as uncompro-

mising in pursuing their goal, which was to spread the influence of a minority Islamic sect called Ismailism. The organization was founded by Hassan-i-Sabbah, who was born in the city of Qom in northern Iran. By the year 1080, he had embarked on a mission to convert the world to Ismailism. Hassan traveled to Egypt to receive religious instruction and then wandered throughout the Middle East seeking converts.

Because the Ismailis were a small and persecuted minority in Islam, Hassan operated in secrecy, becoming a master of disguise to infiltrate communities, build up trust, and lure young men to his cause. He forced recruits to swear an oath of secrecy, convincing them that if they broke their word, they would fall out of favor with Allah (the Islamic name for God) and be denied entry into heaven when they died. On the other hand, if they kept their vows, they would be rewarded with a glorious afterlife in paradise. With a growing band of followers, Hassan worked his way north into territories controlled by the Turkish Empire. By this time, he had had a number of violent skirmishes with the Turkish sultan's armies and had perfected the clandestine, hit-and-run techniques of guerrilla warfare. In 1090, he captured a castle on top of a mountain called Alamut, near his home in northern Iran, where he established a secure base of operations.

Hassan vowed to take revenge on those who had persecuted him and his fellow Ismailis. Realizing he did not have enough men to challenge the sultan's powerful armies in face-to-face combat, he resorted to terrorism, particularly assassination, in a bid to undermine popular confidence in the strength of the Turkish Empire. He hoped to spark a series of popular uprisings among those who had accepted the Ismaili faith. The Assassins' first act of terrorism occurred in 1092, when a young man from Alamut disguised himself as a beggar and stabbed to death a Turkish official named Nizam al-Mulk. The killing was the beginning of a concerted terrorist campaign that lasted for the rest of Hassan's life, and was carried on for several hundred years by his successors at Alamut.

Hassan was ruthless and single-minded, foreshadowing later terrorist leaders who were prepared to sacrifice the amenities of a normal life to pursue their objectives. In his book *The Assassins of Alamut*, historian Anthony Campbell says of Hassan, "He remained within his house, writing, thinking, and planning; he is said to have gone out only twice…. At one time, when things were difficult, he is said to have sent his womenfolk away to another castle…and he never brought them back. He had both his sons executed, one for drinking wine, the other on a charge of [unauthorized] murder."[8]

Suicide Missions

Hassan dispatched thousands of his operatives, called *fida'i*, on audacious assassination missions. Few of them returned alive. In order

Hassan conducts an initiation into his cult of murder, manipulating a fanatical disciple with drugs and the promise of eternal life.

to persuade them to accept these assignments, Hassan established a unique method of initiation into his cult of murder. First, he drugged the recruits by having them smoke hashish (the word "assassin" derives from the word "hashashin"—one who smokes hashish). Then, he blindfolded them and led them into a garden described by the Venetian traveler Marco Polo, who heard the story from one of Hassan's successors when he visited Alamut in the late twelfth century, as "ornamented with gold and with likenesses of all that is beautiful on earth.... There were fair ladies there and damsels, the loveliest in the world, unrivaled at playing every sort of instrument and at singing and dancing."[9]

In their drugged state, Hassan convinced the youths, who were between twelve and twenty years old, that they had been transported to heaven and given a glimpse of the splendid life they would enjoy for eternity if they faithfully carried out the suicide missions he had planned for them. "And he gave his men to understand that this garden was Paradise," Polo continues. "That is why he had made it after this pattern, because Mahomet [Muhammad, the founder of Islam] assured the Saracens [Muslims] that those who go to Paradise will have beautiful women to their hearts' content to do their bidding."[10]

Hassan's ploy infused his young recruits with a fanatical spirit of self-sacrifice. Deluded into believing they would spend eternity in the paradise they'd experienced in their drug-induced fantasy, they willingly went to their deaths carrying out their leader's orders. In doing so, they spread terror throughout the

Turkish Empire and on several occasions brought it close to the brink of collapse. However, Hassan died in 1124 with his dream of Ismaili world domination unfulfilled.

Nevertheless, he left behind a disciplined terrorist organization that continued to wreak havoc in the Muslim world for several hundred years. Without Hassan's leadership, the religious fervor that originally inspired the Assassins gradually evaporated, but his successors continued to use the methods of terrorism to repel European invaders from Muslim lands during the Crusades. For example, in 1192 a French crusader, Conrad of Montferrat, was murdered by an Assassin who had disguised himself as a Christian monk. Finally, in 1272, Alamut was overrun by Mongol hordes from the Central Asian steppe and the Assassins ceased to exist.

Hassan-i-Sabbah's legacy to the history of terrorism is twofold. First, he invented the practice of suicide missions. Second, he was an innovative organizer and structured the Assassins in a decentralized way that is still used by terrorists today. At the top of the hierarchy was the grand master (Hassan himself and his successors at Alamut). Under his guidance, a series of grand priors supervised activities in particular districts. After these came propagandists, who were responsible for recruiting and planning individual acts of terror. Lowest in the hierarchy were the *fida'i*, who carried out the assassinations, often unaware until the last minute of the details of when and where they were to strike. Osama bin Laden, accused of orchestrating the terrorist attacks on the World Trade Center and

The Thuggees

A peculiar brand of terrorism flourished in India from the sixth century A.D. until the mid-1800s. The Thuggee movement (the English word *thug* is derived from the name) was inspired by the worship of Kali, the Hindu goddess of death and destruction. Its members were, for most of the year, respectable merchants and traders who distinguished themselves by devotion to their families and outstanding service to their communities. But every October, Thuggees donned disguises, assembled in bands of between ten and two hundred, and went on a rampage of terror. They preyed on wealthy travelers, whom they robbed and strangled with scarves (Thuggees were also called Phansigers, an ancient Indian word meaning "strangler"). They did not keep all the loot for themselves, distributing most of the spoils among the poor.

Because of their ingenious use of disguise—they often posed as Hindu or Buddhist monks—the Thuggees escaped detection for centuries. It was only when their activities began to threaten the stability of the British colonial regime in the nineteenth century that a concerted effort was made to eradicate them.

Membership in the Thuggees was hereditary. In an article in the *Yale Journal of Criticism* titled "Discovering India, Imagining Thuggee," Parama Roy quotes a Thuggee called Bukhtawar telling a British tribunal: "I am a Thug[g]ee, my father and grandfather were Thug[g]ees." They were drawn together by their devotion to Kali, a fierce goddess with multiple arms, often portrayed wearing a garland of skulls around her neck and brandishing a bloody sword in one of her many hands. Before each murder, the Thuggees enacted a ritual in which they ate sugar symbolizing the body of Kali. They always strangled their victims with a scarf called a *rumal* and buried the bodies in shallow graves dug with a specific kind of pickax, which they then used as a grave marker to publicize their acts of terror. The Thuggees employed an intricate system of clandestine signs to let each other know they were members of the cult and even evolved a secret language to exchange information.

The Thuggees took advantage of religious superstition to spread their brand of terror. They encouraged the belief that the rash of murders that took place every autumn was the result of Kali's displeasure. The tactic engendered so much fear that people often went into hiding during the killing season to escape the wrath of the furious and vengeful goddess. The British administration regarded the Thuggees as a challenge to their rule. Parama Roy quotes historian David Arnold: "To the colonial regime, crime and politics were almost inseparable: serious crime was an implicit defiance of state authority and a possible prelude to rebellion." In 1828, the British appointed Captain William Sleeman to ferret out the Thuggees. By 1848, more than three thousand of them had been arrested or hanged. Many went to their deaths on the gallows loudly declaring their devotion to Kali and dedicating their murderous careers to her honor.

the Pentagon on September 11, 2001, publicly acknowledged the debt he owed to the organizational scheme created by Hassan.

The Reign of Terror

Terrorism did not play a significant role in the political and military events of the Middle Ages and the early modern eras, but it erupted in a new form in the last decade of the eighteenth century. France was in the grip of an economic crisis caused, in part, by the excesses of the extravagant court of King Louis XVI and his queen, Marie Antoinette.

The peasantry and the growing middle class were clamoring for the king to reform the tax system and reduce the national debt, but Louis was either incapable or unwilling to comply. The Estates General, an assembly with representatives from all classes, was convened in 1789; it called for a reduction in the king's powers and the implementation of democratic reforms.

While the king and the assembly negotiated, the people became increasingly impatient. A mob stormed the Bastille, a fortress on the eastern edge of Paris, and several

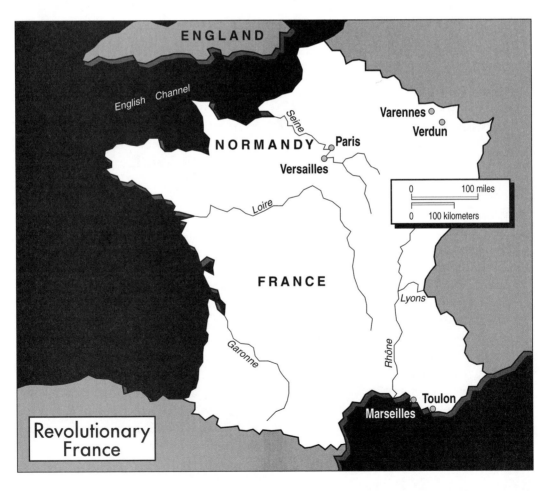

Revolutionary France

short-lived peasant uprisings in the countryside occurred. Louis continued to waver, and the Estates General, now called the National Assembly, wrested power from his hands and put him and Marie Antoinette under arrest. Under pressure from the peasants and the middle class, the assembly instituted sweeping democratic reforms. Foreign monarchies, worried that the spirit of revolution would cross their borders, joined with Louis's supporters in France to oppose the new government. Months of instability ended when the assembly appointed a twelve-man Committee of Public Safety to run the country.

An influential member of the committee was Maximilien Robespierre, a lawyer who used his considerable oratorical skills to urge that enemies of the revolution—both inside and outside France—be suppressed no matter what the cost in money and lives. Robespierre dominated the committee, undertook the direct supervision of the military and the judiciary, and effectively assumed control of the new government. He reorganized the army and sent troops to defend the country's borders from the external threat. When that was accomplished, he turned his attention to the internal foes of the revolution, launching a nationwide campaign of repression that became known as the Reign of Terror.

Inspired by Robespierre's fiery rhetoric, a mob attacked the Tuileries Palace in Paris, where the king was under house arrest. The royal family escaped, but six hundred guards were hacked to death by the frenzied rioters. The National Assembly put the king on trial

Maximilien Robespierre, architect of the campaign that became known as the Reign of Terror.

for treason against the French people. Louis was found guilty by a margin of one vote, and he and Marie Antionette were publicly executed while a crowd of thousands cheered.

The Guillotine

The deaths of Louis and Marie Antoinette whetted the thirst for blood. On September 5, 1793, the National Assembly approved the Reign of Terror as its official policy and gave Robespierre a free hand to rid France of all

The guillotine, a symbol of the Reign of Terror, brought death to more than seventeen thousand condemned prisoners.

opposition to the revolution. In an impassioned speech, he defended the use of terror to shore up the fragile new government. "We must smother the internal and external enemies of the Republic or perish with it," Robespierre told the National Assembly.

> In this situation, the first maxim of your policy ought to be to lead the people by reason and the people's enemies by terror. If the spring of popular government in time of peace is virtue, the springs of popular government in revolution are at once virtue and terror. Terror is nothing other than justice, prompt, severe, inflexible; it is therefore an emanation [outgrowth] of virtue; it is not so much a special principle as it is a consequence of the general principle of democracy applied to our country's most urgent needs.[11]

During the Reign of Terror, more than 250,000 people were arbitrarily arrested by troops dispatched throughout the country by Robespierre. Some of these arrests were individuals genuinely conspiring to undermine the authority of the government, but thousands of others were jailed simply on suspicion of having expressed critical opinions. They were brought before hastily assembled tribunals without the benefit of legal representation or the opportunity to defend themselves. Many were condemned by hearsay evidence that they were not allowed to challenge. More than seventeen thousand of these people had their heads cut off on the guillotine, which became a symbol of the Reign of Terror. Many more died at the hands of angry mobs who dispensed vigilante justice with the silent assent of Robespierre's government. Entire families were jailed, even if only one member was accused of wrongdoing. In one horrifying incident, an executed widower's two sons were sent to the guillotine simply because there would be no one left to take care of them after his death. The atrocities terrorized the populace into meek submission. Eager to ingratiate themselves with the authorities, many falsely accused their friends and neighbors of antigovernment activities or attitudes, adding to the number of innocent French men and women who were led to the guillotine.

To critics of the brutality, who accused the allegedly democratic government of being no better than the autocratic monarchy it replaced, Robespierre replied,

> It has been said that terror is the principle of despotic government. Does your government therefore resemble despotism? Yes, as the sword that gleams in the hands of the heroes of liberty resembles that with which the henchmen of tyranny are armed. Let the despot govern by terror his brutalized subjects; he is right as a despot. Subdue by terror the enemies of liberty, and you will be right as founders of the Republic. The government of the revolution is liberty's despotism against tyranny. . . . Indulgence for the royalists, cry certain men, mercy for the villains! No![12]

The Terror Turns on Its Creator

Once unleashed, the Reign of Terror proved impossible to control. As the level of violence rose, opposition became more fervent and repression more intense. Historians estimate that approximately forty thousand people fell victim to the guillotine or died at the hands of angry mobs. Of these, less than 15 percent were members of the nobility, the faction most earnestly trying to restore a monarchical form of government; the rest were peasants and middle-class artisans and businessmen, in whose name the revolution was being fought.

Other nations looked on with horror at the bloodbath that was unfolding in France. British political theorist Edmund Burke, who had supported the American Revolution less than two decades earlier, railed against what he felt to be a betrayal of the principles of democracy. Speaking of the leadership, including Robespierre, he said,

> Not one drop of their blood have they shed in the cause of the country they have ruined. They have made no sacrifices to their projects of greater consequence than their shoe buckles, whilst they were imprisoning their king, murdering their fellow citizens, and bathing in tears, and plunging in poverty and distress, thousands of worthy men and worthy families. Their cruelty [has authorized] treasons, robberies, rapes, assassinations, slaughters, and burnings throughout their harassed land.[13]

Burke did not foresee that Robespierre was about to pay the ultimate sacrifice for the excesses of his Reign of Terror. He turned against his fellow members of the Committee of Public Safety and ordered the execution of several people he suspected of conspiring

The Reign of Terror ended with Robespierre's execution.

dank jail cell, holding his shattered jaw together with his hands. On the morning of July 28, 1794, he was led to the guillotine and executed. Robespierre's death brought the Reign of Terror to an end, but the rampage of violence left the French Revolution in chaos. Within five years, the experiment in democracy was over, and the people gratefully turned control over to a dictator, Napoléon Bonaparte, who ruled as autocratically as the king they had deposed.

The Reign of Terror was a watershed event in the history of terrorism. Previous terrorist activity was carried out against governments; this time, the government was the perpetrator. It was, says political scientist Albert Parry,

against him. Hearing of his intentions, however, they struck first and had him arrested and dragged from the floor of the National Assembly. Robespierre's supporters exchanged gunfire with the troops sent to detain him, and a bullet struck him in the face. The instigator of the Reign of Terror spent his last night in a

history's first campaign of political terror to be legislated by a people's duly elected representatives into a state-authorized system. And so, though terror had been used by individuals and groups before Robespierre's rule, his Reign of Terror systematized violence, hallowed it by the state's prestige, and created an intense fear in a way and on a scale heretofore unknown, a way that gave rise to the concept of modern terrorism.[14]

Chapter Two

Propaganda of the Bomb

The French Revolution failed to establish democratic government on a firm foundation, and following Napoléon's rise to power, Europe's autocratic regimes enjoyed a brief respite from attack. But by the mid–nineteenth century, the continent was once again in turmoil. Monarchies, weakened by outmoded economic and social policies, were under increasing pressure to institute reforms. In country after country, peaceful democratic movements were either ignored or repressed. In 1848, violent uprisings erupted in France, Germany, Italy, and a number of other nations. These revolutions were quickly put down, but they left behind a hunger for more freedom and democracy.

Anarchism

The political discontent that swept Europe spawned a political philosophy called anarchism. The primary tenet of anarchism was the belief that injustice and inequality were caused by the state, which was thought to be little more than an instrument to support and defend the interests of the privileged classes. The establishment of a just society, the anarchists held, depended on the destruction of the state, especially those branches of it—the military and the police—that enforced domination over the masses. It was believed that once the state was brought down, people would govern themselves, wealth would be equally distributed, and justice and prosperity would reign.

Anarchists differed on the exact social, economic, and political form this self-governance would take, but they were unanimous on one thing: The state must be overthrown, by violent means if necessary. In this, the anarchists agreed with Karl Marx, whose revolutionary political philosophy was beginning to

Terrorism and Marxism

Many terrorist groups have claimed allegiance to the revolutionary Communist philosophy of Karl Marx. However, orthodox Marxists have in fact always repudiated terrorism. Leon Trotsky, one of the principal theoreticians of the Marxist-inspired Russian Revolution of 1917, points out that terrorism is contrary to the Marxist goal of organizing a mass uprising of the working class to replace the capitalist economic system with socialism. Marxists, he acknowledges, are not opposed to violence, but isolated acts of terrorism fail to accomplish lasting social, political, and economic change because they distract members of the working class from the discipline and patience required for a lengthy class struggle. Instead, terrorism conditions them to think that a small, elite group of highly committed commandos will do the work—and take the risks—for them. Trotsky explains the Marxist position on terrorism in this excerpt from his 1909 book, Why Marxists Oppose Individual Terrorism.

"Only the conscious and organized working class can . . . look out for proletarian [worker] interests. However, in order to murder a prominent official you need not have the organized masses behind you. The recipe for explosives is accessible to all, and a Browning [a type of rifle] can be obtained anywhere. In the first case, there is a social struggle, whose methods and means flow necessarily from the nature of the prevailing social order; and in the second, a purely mechanical reaction . . . very striking in its outward form (murder, explosions and so forth) but absolutely harmless as far as the social system goes. . . .

The capitalist state does not base itself on government ministers and cannot be eliminated with them. The classes it serves will always find new people; the mechanism remains intact and continues to function. But the disarray introduced into the ranks of the working masses themselves by a terrorist attempt is much deeper. If it is enough to arm oneself with a pistol in order to achieve one's goal, why the efforts of the class struggle? . . . The smoke from the confusion clears away, the panic disappears, the successor of the murdered minister makes his appearance, life again settles into the old rut, the wheel of capitalist exploitation turns as before; only the police repression grows more savage and brazen. And as a result, in place of the kindled hopes and artificially aroused excitement comes disillusionment and apathy."

Karl Marx called for a mass uprising of the working class.

gain support among members of the working class.

Both Marx and the anarchists believed that workers, as the class most oppressed by the prevailing system, would lead the revolution. But first the workers would have to be motivated to organize themselves into a fighting force. Marx argued that this could best be accomplished by patient, peaceful propaganda—speeches, pamphlets, and educational programs promoting political awareness. Most anarchists, on the other hand, felt that the working class, because its members were poorly educated, would be more likely to respond to less intellectual means of instruction. Thus was born the idea of "propaganda of the deed" or "propaganda of the bomb." Workers would be galvanized into action when they saw a concrete demonstration of the state's vulnerability to violent attack. Individual acts of terror, especially the assassination of public figures and the bombing of public facilities, would be the spark that ignited mass uprising.

The Russian anarchist Nikolai Morozov predicted that terrorism would spread revolutionary fervor throughout society. "The goal of the terroristic movement . . . should make the struggle popular [widespread]," he wrote. "It should bring the way of the struggle into the lives of the people in such a manner that every new appearance of tyranny in the future will be met by new groups of people . . . and these groups will destroy oppression by consecutive political assassinations. . . . Terroristic struggle will merge into one wide stream and then no despotism or brutal force will be able to stand up against it."[15]

Terrorism and Morality

The nineteenth-century European terrorists, like those in other times and places, regarded their acts of violence as an ethically legitimate form of self-defense against the brutality of tyranny. The anarchists argued that the state itself, through its police forces and armies, employed violence or the threat of violence to subjugate the lower classes. Therefore, they maintained, terror was necessary for history to progress toward freedom and justice for all.

In 1849, German radical Karl Heinzen published an influential book called *Evolution* in which he described terrorism as a requirement of social change. The end, he insisted, justified the means:

> Let us now . . . spell out in plain speech what the lesson is which is now being illustrated every day before our eyes in the form of actions and threats, blood and torture, cannons and gallows by both princes and freedom-fighters . . . to wit, that murder is the principal agent of historical progress. We take as our fundamental principle, taught us by our enemies, that murder, both of individuals and masses, is still a necessity, an unavoidable instrument in the achievement of historical ends. . . . Once killing has been accepted, the moral stance is seen to have no foundation, the legal is seen as ineffectual, and the political is alone of any significance. Is the end achieved? This is the only question which you cultivators and organizers of murder [the state] permit us to ask

The Ku Klux Klan

The end of the American Civil War saw the beginnings of a right-wing terrorist movement in the South that continues, although in diminished form, to the present day. The Ku Klux Klan was founded by a handful of defeated Confederate army officers in Pulaski, Tennessee, in 1866. Initially, it was little more than a social club.

Klansmen hide their identity using sheets and white hoods.

The character of the Klan changed quickly, however. The post–Civil War South was in the grip of an economic crisis. Unemployment was high, and there was seething resentment against African Americans who were taking advantage of their newfound freedom from slavery to enter the labor market and compete with whites for scarce jobs. Numerous discontented Southerners joined the Klan and transformed it into a terrorist organization that preyed on African Americans and their white sympathizers.

The Klan staged nighttime raids. Dressed in white sheets and hoods and riding horses, they would descend on their victim amid the thunder of pounding hooves, put a rope around his neck, and drag him from his home. Thousands of beatings, mutilations, lynchings, burnings, and bombings were reported, but Klan members largely escaped prosecution because they enjoyed widespread sympathy in the white community. They accented their brand of terror by planting flaming crosses at the sites of their atrocities. The fiery cross became a symbol that drove many African Americans from the South into northern cities and intimidated many southern officials, preventing them from taking action to stop Klan violence.

The Klan lost a large number of members after the federal government adopted a hard-line policy toward secret organizations in 1871, but it regrouped in 1915 as the Invisible Knights of the Ku Klux Klan. Klansmen, wearing their trademark white sheets and hoods, marauded through states not only in the South but in the Midwest and the Northeast. They continued to employ violent, secret tactics, but they also held large public rallies to spread their message of white supremacism and racial and religious intolerance.

The Klan supported Adolf Hitler's rise to power in Germany in the 1930s, and there is some evidence that it received funding from the Nazi Party. When America joined the war effort in 1941, the Klan's Nazi affiliation caused many members to defect. It disbanded as a national organization in 1944. Since then, it has continued as a number of small, uncoordinated cells that hold sporadic rallies at which their leaders spew hatred to dwindling numbers of like-minded bigots.

ourselves, by forcing us to adopt your theory of murder.... Even if we have to blow up half a continent or spill a sea of blood, in order to finish off the barbarian party, we should have no scruples about doing it.[16]

A Russian revolutionary terrorist, Gerasim Romanenko, attempted to provide another moral justification for terrorism: Because ter-

---

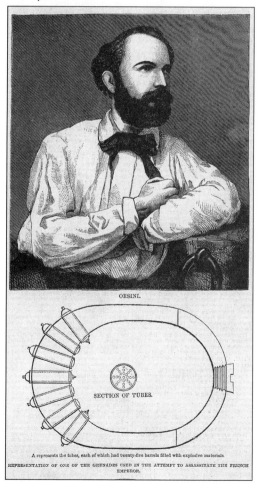

Anarchist Felice Orsini and a drawing of the bomb device used in the attempted assassination of Napoleon III.

ORSINI.

SECTION OF TUBES.

A represents the tubes, each of which had twenty-five barrels filled with explosive materials.

REPRESENTATION OF ONE OF THE GRENADES USED IN THE ATTEMPT TO ASSASSINATE THE FRENCH EMPEROR.

---

rorists were selective in their choice of targets, limiting their victims to political leaders and other influential people, their acts of violence shed less blood than the indiscriminate killing of full-scale class warfare as envisioned by Marx and his followers. In Romanenko's view, says historian Walter Laqueur, "terrorism was not only effective, it was humanitarian. It cost infinitely fewer victims than a mass struggle; in a popular revolution the best were killed while the real villains looked on from the sidelines. The blows of terrorism were directed against the main culprits; a few innocent people might suffer, but this was inevitable in warfare."[17]

Finally, terrorism was justified on the grounds of its efficiency. A few assassinations, bombings, and poisonings would spread terror throughout society, undermining the authority of the ruling elite. "The revolutionaries must try to bring about a situation where the barbarians [the ruling class] are afraid for their lives every hour of the day or night," Heinzen wrote. "They must think that every drink of water, every mouthful of food, every bed, every bush, every paving stone ... may be a killer. For them as for us, may fear be the herald and murder the executioner."[18]

Decades of Violence

The call to terroristic violence issued by the anarchists sparked a wave of bombings and assassinations throughout Europe and America that lasted through the rest of the nineteenth century and into the early years of the twentieth. Although the murder of kings and other social leaders is as old as civilization, the attempted assassination of French emperor Napoléon III by an anarchist named Felice Orsini in 1858 marked the beginning of modern terrorism. It was, says Duke University's Martin Miller, the first assassination in modern times "to be carried out for explicitly political reasons [the Zealots and Assassins used political means to achieve essentially religious objectives, and the Reign of Terror was designed to cement the power of the state] as part of a secret transnational conspiracy in the context of simultaneously creating an atmosphere of intimidation and fear in the general society."[19]

Before carrying out his attack, Orsini assembled an international network of accomplices that stretched from Italy to England and included explosive experts, military tacticians, and political advisers. He bought bombs from a factory in Manchester, England, and had them smuggled into France by his cohorts. On the night of January 14, 1858, Orsini and two accomplices waited outside a Paris opera house for the arrival of Emperor Napoléon and Empress Eugenie. As the imperial carriage drew up in front of the building, three bombs were thrown, creating a devastating explosion. The emperor and his wife escaped with minor injuries, but 156 people were wounded. Eight of the victims, including a thirteen-year-old boy, died in the blast.

The deaths of innocent bystanders provoked a reaction throughout France that was part outrage and part insecurity. It was, says Miller, "the moment in which modern terrorism became an operational reality and a permanent characteristic of Western society."[20] It was also the first of a staggering number of terrorist attacks to plague Europe and

America. Before the wave of anarchist terror subsided, the kings of Italy and Spain, the czar of Russia, the empress of Austria, the prime minister of France, and President William McKinley of the United States fell victim to assassination. Scores of lower-level government officials also died in the rash of attacks, and the number of innocent casualties reached into the thousands.

The advances in weapons technology that put bombs at the disposal of terrorists made it inevitable that blameless bystanders would be injured in their attacks. As the number of such casualties increased, advocates of terrorism could no longer plausibly claim, as Romanenko had tried to do, that terrorism was totally selective in its targets. But they attempted to shift the blame by blurring the distinction between the guilty and the innocent, arguing—questionably—that anyone who benefited from social and economic inequality was tainted. In March 1894, Emil Henry, a well-known anarchist, detonated a bomb in the crowded St. Lazare railway station in Paris in retaliation for the execution a week earlier of one of his associates. One person was killed and nineteen were badly injured by Henry's bomb. When it was pointed out at his trial that he had imperiled the lives of women and children, shop clerks and workers, and others who were not guilty of any of the crimes of which he accused the ruling class, Henry defiantly responded:

There are no innocents. [Anarchists] do not spare bourgeois [middle-class] women and children because the wives and children of those they [the anarchists] love are not spared either. Are not those children innocent victims who, in the slums, die slowly of aneaemia because bread is scarce at home; or those women who grow pale in your workshops and wear themselves out to earn 40 sous [cents] a day, and yet are lucky when poverty does not turn them into prostitutes?[21]

Terror Invades America

Anarchist terrorism provoked violent repression on the part of European governments, and many terrorists who escaped prison or execution fled to America, where they allied themselves with the trade unions.

The American labor movement had already experienced incidents of terrorism. The Molly Maguires, a secret organization formed by Irish coal miners in Pennsylvania, conducted a campaign of terror against company bosses during the decade between 1865 and 1875. The Maguires tried to intimidate mine owners by assassinating managers, destroying property, and fighting armed battles with strike breakers and police. Violence spread to other parts of the country after 1873, when a severe economic recession caused massive nationwide unemployment.

It was into this environment of labor unrest that Johann Most arrived in 1882.

Thousands of angry unionists attack police at Chicago's Haymarket Square Massacre in 1886.

Most was a German machinist and a rabid anarchist who had been driven from Europe because of his outspoken support of terrorists in France and England as well as in his native land. In New York, he established a radical newspaper and preached labor violence at worker gatherings. He published instructions on bomb making and terrorist tactics and exerted considerable influence in the labor movement, especially among immigrant workers.

Most had a large contingent of followers in Chicago, many of whom joined in a nationwide strike in 1886 demanding higher wages and a shorter workweek. On May 3, Chicago police fired into a crowd of strikers at the McCormick Harvester Plant, killing one and seriously wounding several others. A union newspaper, the *Alarm*, with which Most was associated, called for the strikers to stage a protest.

On May 4, three thousand workers gathered at Chicago's Haymarket Square. While they were listening to speeches, two contingents of police arrived to disperse them. As both sides faced each other in an uneasy standoff, an unknown terrorist threw a bomb into the group of police, who retaliated by shooting into the crowd of workers. Seven policemen died, and an unrecorded number of workers were killed and wounded. The next day, police raided union offices, arresting hundreds in a citywide crackdown. Despite flimsy evidence, seven unionists were sentenced to death for their role in what had come to be called the Haymarket Square Massacre. Most was sentenced to a year in jail for inciting labor violence.

Anarchist Assassination

Anarchism inspired other acts of terror in the American labor movement. With Most in jail, a young Russian-born anarchist, Alexander Berkman, came to the forefront. Berkman was incensed when guards hired by the Carnegie Steel Company to put down a strike at its Pittsburgh plant shot several workers to death. To retaliate, Berkman concealed a small explosive device in his mouth, stormed into the office of Carnegie executive William Clay Frick, and tried to detonate the tiny bomb with his teeth, perhaps staging history's first suicide bombing attempt. The bomb failed to explode and Berkman, subdued by Frick's bodyguards, spent the next two decades in prison.

Alexander Berkman (background) storms the office of Carnegie executive William Clay Frick.

Leon Czolgosz did not belong to any radical organizations, but he was an avid reader of anarchist literature. The mill worker from Cleveland was especially impressed by the writings of an anarchist firebrand named Emma Goldman; he devoured her pamphlets and traveled to hear her speeches whenever he could. In 1898, Czolgosz experienced a nervous breakdown and became obsessed with the idea of political violence. When Italy's King Humbert I was murdered by an anarchist gunman, Czolgosz decided that he would attempt to spread terror in America by assassinating President William McKinley.

With cold detachment, Czolgosz bought a short-barreled revolver and journeyed to Buffalo, New York, where McKinley was due to give a speech on September 6, 1901. Even though security had been increased due to a number of recent terrorist incidents, the disturbed twenty-eight-year-old managed to get into a line of well-wishers waiting to shake the president's hand. With his weapon wrapped in a scarf, Czolgosz bided his time as the line slowly advanced. When his turn came, he brushed aside McKinley's extended hand and fired two shots. Eight days later, the president died of his wounds. The nation was shocked that not even the chief executive was safe from terrorist violence. Czolgosz was quickly tried and executed.

Other assassinations followed, including the bombing death in 1905 of Frank Steunenberg, a former governor of Idaho. His assailant was Albert Horsley, a member of a radical miners' union who confessed to committing other acts of terrorism on the union's behalf, including twenty-six murders. In 1916, labor

Leon Czolgosz (center left) shoots President McKinley with a concealed revolver.

agitators were blamed for throwing a bomb into a parade in San Francisco, killing ten and injuring forty. The terrorist killings, especially that of McKinley, plunged America into a "Red scare," an irrational fear that Communists and anarchists were poised to launch a violent revolution. Government agents rounded up hundreds of radicals and their sympathizers. Emma Goldman and Johann Most were caught in the dragnet. Goldman was deported to her native Russia. Most was released on the condition that he curtail his political activities.

Terrorism, Revolution, and World War

Terrorism played a major role in the Communist revolution in Russia, although the leaders of that world-altering event repudiated its tactics. In 1879, a small group of intellectuals, inspired by anarchist theories of social change, formed an organization called the People's Will. Their goal was to strike at the repressive regime of Czar Alexander II through a series of political assassinations. In this they were successful, helping to undermine the czar's authoritarian rule and pave the way for the Marxist revolution that finally toppled the government in 1917.

Dozens of regional governors and other officials of the czar's administration fell to the bombs and bullets of the People's Will, but the organization's most dramatic act of terrorism was the assassination of Czar Alexander himself. The head of the death squad was a twenty-six-year-old woman named Sofia Perovskaya, whose lover had been arrested just days before in a failed attempt on the czar's life. On March 13, 1881, Perovskaya and three accomplices armed with bombs placed themselves at points along the route that Alexander's carriage normally followed to and from his palace in St. Petersburg. Alexander, aware that plotters were trying to kill him, changed his route at the last minute, but Perovskaya had prepared herself thoroughly and figured out which of many alternative routes was the most likely. She quickly ordered her team of assassins to the new location. As the czar's carriage passed by, one of the terrorists rolled a bomb among

Gavrilo Princip fires a gun at Austro-Hungarian archduke Franz Ferdinand.

the horses' hooves. It exploded with a deafening blast, but left Alexander unhurt. As the czar surveyed the damage, he was heard thanking God for sparing his life. At that moment, a second terrorist threw a bomb directly at him, killing him. The bomber also sustained fatal injuries. Perovskaya and three others were arrested and hanged.

Scholars agree that the First World War would have happened without the intervention of Gavrilo Princip, but they concede that it would not have started exactly when it did had the Serbian terrorist not assassinated Austro-Hungarian archduke Franz Ferdinand in the Bosnian capital of Sarajevo on June 28,

1914. The motive for this last of the nineteenth- and early twentieth-century wave of anarchist-inspired acts of terrorism was Serbian freedom from domination by the Austro-Hungarian Empire.

There were twenty assassins involved in the plot. One of them, Borijove Jevtic, describes the incident, as the archduke's open car approached a turn in the road: "Princip stepped forward from the curb, drew his automatic pistol from his coat and fired two shots. The first struck the wife of the Archduke, the Archduchess Sofia, in the abdomen. She was an expectant mother. She died instantly. The second bullet struck the Archduke close to the heart. He uttered one word, 'Sofia'—a call to his stricken wife. Then his head fell back and he collapsed. He died almost instantly."[22] Sentenced to death for the shooting, Princip told the governor of the prison where he was being held: "I suggest you nail me to a cross and burn me alive. My flaming body will be a torch to light my people on their path to freedom."[23]

Ironically, Franz Ferdinand was not chosen as a target because he supported repressive policies against the Serbs. Rather, says historian Walter Laqueur, "The Serbian Black Hand [the terrorist group to which Princip belonged] decided to kill Archduke Franz Ferdinand not because they regarded him as particularly wicked but, on the contrary, because they were afraid that he would make political concessions, thus weakening the spirit of the nationalist movement."[24] This fact highlights an aspect of terrorist strategy that analysts of more recent events have frequently misunderstood. Often, terrorist acts are inspired by a desire to make the political situation worse, not better, hoping that authorities will overreact and thus inadvertently help the terrorists' cause. This was the case in the assassination of Archduke Ferdinand, and it helped to precipitate World War I.

Chapter Three

Anticolonial Terrorism

The advent of World War I drove terrorism into the background as the armies of Europe and America clashed in an eruption of violence that dwarfed anything terrorists, with their limited resources, could hope to accomplish. In the years between the end of the First and Second World Wars (1918 to 1945), terrorism by individuals and small groups was eclipsed by the repressive state terror of Nazi Germany, with its death camps, and Communist dictator Joseph Stalin's Russia, where millions of dissenters were imprisoned or killed. But with the end of World War II there was a resurgence of terrorist activity on the part of peoples who felt compelled to resort to violence to free themselves from the colonial domination of foreign governments. Colonialism describes a phenomenon that goes back to the early modern era, when European states used their naval and military might to impose their rule on territories in other parts of the world. By the mid–twentieth century, the colonial system was beginning to break down, but the process was slow and a number of colonized peoples were growing impatient for the right to govern themselves. When negotiation failed, they turned to terrorism to drive the colonial powers from their shores.

Broken Promises

The British captured Palestine from the Turkish Ottoman Empire in 1918. The area was populated mostly by Arabs, but there was also a small number of Jews, who had settled in their traditional biblical homeland to escape ethnic and religious persecution in Europe. The British sowed seeds of future discontent by making contradictory promises to both the Arabs and the Jews: To the Arabs they had promised independence in exchange for help in fighting the Turks;

to the Jews they promised a national home in Palestine. Jewish immigration to Palestine increased during the 1920s. The Palestinian Arabs, outraged that the British appeared to be giving their land away, began sporadic attacks on Jewish settlements.

In 1922, the British tried to placate the Palestinians by limiting Jewish immigration. At the same time, they affirmed their commitment to the establishment of a Jewish state, without, however, specifying exactly what territory such a state would occupy. Even though this policy satisfied neither side, it was approved by the League of Nations (an international association of countries that was a precursor to the United Nations) and

became known as the British Mandate in Palestine.

Tension between the Jews and Palestinians rose sharply after Hitler seized power in Germany in the 1930s. To escape the Nazi regime's brutal anti-Semitism, many thousands of Jews fled to Palestine. The Palestinians responded by increasing the intensity of their attacks on Jewish settlements. When the British tried to restore order by blocking further immigration, the Jews began to smuggle refugees from Germany into Palestine in defiance of the ban.

In 1942, while the Second World War raged in Europe, Britain, along with a number of other nations, signed a pact agreeing

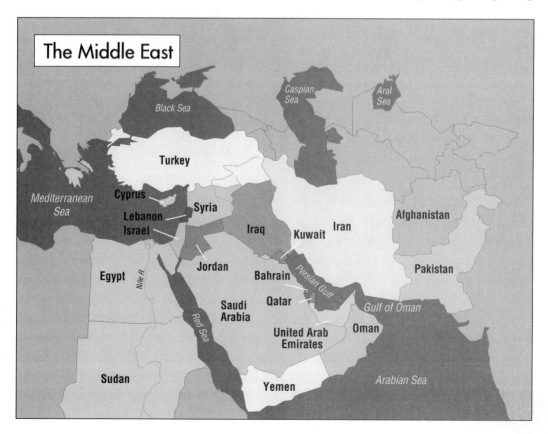

The Middle East

Black Sea

Caspian Sea

Aral Sea

Turkey

Mediterranean Sea

Cyprus

Syria

Lebanon

Israel

Iraq

Kuwait

Iran

Afghanistan

Egypt

Nile R.

Jordan

Bahrain

Persian Gulf

Pakistan

Saudi Arabia

Qatar

Gulf of Oman

United Arab Emirates

Oman

Red Sea

Sudan

Yemen

Arabian Sea

From Terrorist to Statesman

Menachem Begin, head of the Jewish terrorist organization Irgun during the 1940s, served as prime minister of Israel from 1977 to 1983, and in 1979 signed the first peace treaty between Israel and an Arab government (Egypt). In this passage from his book The Revolt *(quoted in* The Terrorism Reader, *edited by Walter Laqueur and Yonah Alexander), Begin describes how his experiences leading a secretive, underground terrorist operation helped prepare him to become a head of state.*

"A fighting underground is a veritable state in miniature: a state at war. It has its army, its police, its own courts. It has at its disposal all the executive arms of a state. Above all, it bore the responsibility for life-and-death not only for individuals, but for whole generations. Nor is it only in this sense that an underground resembles a state. Just as in the ministries and departments of government, so too in the underground and its divisions and sections, there is cooperation and there are quarrels, arising from human nature itself.... It is no exaggeration to say that in the underground we all gained some experience of the machinery of state, with its light and shadows, its virtues and defects."

Menachem Begin once led the Jewish terrorist organization Irgun.

not to implement in their colonies "territorial changes that do not accord with the freely expressed wishes of the peoples concerned" and to "respect the right of all peoples to choose the form of government under which they will live."[25] Acting on these principles, the Jews in Palestine demanded the right to form their own government. When the British refused, the Jews initiated a campaign of terrorism.

The revolt against British rule was "waged by two small Jewish terrorist organizations," says terrorism expert Bruce Hoffman, "the Irgun Zvai Le'umi (National Military Organization, or Irgun) and the Lohamei Herut Yisrael (Freedom Fighters for Israel, known to Jews by its Hebrew acronym Lehi, and to the British as the Stern Gang). The Irgun's campaign was the more significant of the two, in that it established a revolutionary model which thereafter was emulated by…terrorist groups around the world."[26] The Irgun began as a defense squad to protect Jewish settlements from Arab attack. It progressed to staging retaliatory strikes against the Arabs and then became a full-fledged terrorist group, targeting the British army and officials of the colonial administration.

Bombs and Publicity

The terrorists were small in number, never more than several hundred active members, and their relationship with the political leaders of the Jewish community in Palestine was ambivalent. On the one hand, the leadership advocated peaceful negotiation with the British; on the other, they welcomed the armed protection the terrorists offered against the Arabs. In general, the mood among the Jews in Palestine was militant and quietly supportive of terrorist activity: They were well aware of the atrocities being committed in Nazi Germany and that, historically, the Jews had been the helpless victims of persecution many times before. David Ben-Gurion, who became Israel's first prime minister in 1948, was one leader who espoused such beliefs. He opposed terrorism, yet in 1943, he said, "We had lived a life of exile in foreign lands, a life

Irgun troops march through the streets of Tel Aviv in 1948.

of dependence, shame, slavery, and disgrace; not only caused by others, but also by ourselves, as a result of our acceptance of our weakness.... From now on, we shall guarantee a new death for ourselves, not a death of weakness, helplessness, and futile sacrifice. We shall die with arms in our hands."[27]

The Irgun was headed by Menachem Begin, a lawyer and a former private in the Polish army, who had escaped from the European Holocaust. He was enraged at the British policy limiting immigration and preventing other persecuted Jews from fleeing the Nazi death camps. "As a lowly enlisted man...with only a bare minimum of formal military training, Begin was an unlikely strategist," says Bruce Hoffman. "But he possessed an uncanny analytical ability to cut right to the heart of an issue and an intuitive sense about the interplay between violence, politics and propaganda that ideally qualified him to lead a terrorist organization."[28]

The Irgun carried out bombings of British installations, both military and civilian. Begin insisted that targets with symbolic value be chosen in order to attract maximum media coverage. On a single day in 1944, Irgun commandos blew up British administrative offices in Palestine's three major cities—Jerusalem, Tel Aviv, and Haifa. They also bombed land registry offices, which administered the British policy restricting the immigration of Jews. The group pioneered the use of the letter bomb, or package bomb, delivering explosives under the guise of innocent correspondence. The Stern Gang, under the leadership of Avram Stern and Yitzak Shamir, split from the Irgun and carried out a campaign of assassination, killing, among others, the British foreign secretary for eastern affairs Lord Moyne and United Nations mediator Folke Bernadotte.

Both groups employed a policy of provocation, hoping their attacks would cause the British to overreact. They believed that the resulting publicity would attract sympathy to the Jewish cause and that, ultimately, the international community would pressure the British to withdraw from Palestine. The terrorists also calculated that press accounts of the struggle would convince the British people that the price of maintaining a colony in Palestine was too high, prompting them to make this feeling known through their votes in elections back home in England.

The End of the Struggle

In July 1946, the Irgun staged a spectacular bombing at the King David Hotel in Jerusalem. Two floors of the south wing had been leased by the British and converted into the headquarters of both the military and civilian branches of their administration in Palestine. Six Irgun operatives disguised as Arab deliverymen entered the hotel through the kitchen entrance and placed seven milk churns packed with TNT and gelignite in the basement just beneath the offices occupied by the colonial officials. The target was the British, not innocent people staying in or working at the hotel. Several minutes before the blast was scheduled to go off, the Irgun telephoned a warning to evacuate the building.

Despite the precautions, when the bomb exploded, ninety-one people were killed and forty-five injured, including Arab and Jewish women and children as well as the British.

King David Hotel bombing, July 1946.

The bombing of the King David was the most devastating single incident of terrorism to that date and it made headlines around the world. It succeeded in weakening support for the British presence in Palestine and caused the British themselves to doubt that they could ever bring peace to the region. Begin explained the role of terrorism in undermining the confidence of the colonial power: "The very existence of an underground must, in the end, undermine the prestige of a colonial regime. Every attack which it fails to prevent is a blow at its standing. Even if the attack does not succeed, it makes a dent in that prestige, and that dent widens into a crack which is extended with every succeeding attack."[29]

As dramatic as the bombing of the King David Hotel was, the terrorist act that finally ensured the withdrawal of the colonial forces from Palestine came a year later, when the Irgun kidnapped and hanged two British sergeants in retaliation for the execution of

43

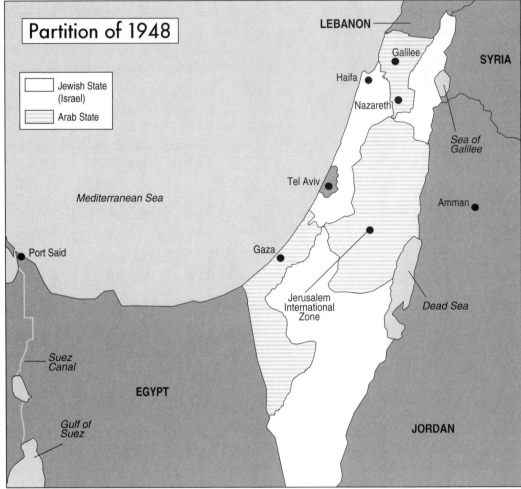

Partition of 1948

Jewish State (Israel)

Arab State

LEBANON

Galilee

SYRIA

Haifa

Nazareth

Sea of Galilee

Tel Aviv

Amman

Mediterranean Sea

Gaza

Jerusalem International Zone

Dead Sea

Port Said

Suez Canal

EGYPT

Gulf of Suez

JORDAN

three Jewish combatants. Pictures of the death scene—the sergeants dangling from a makeshift scaffold, their heads hooded and their shirts bloodied—appeared in every British newspaper and came to symbolize the futility of colonial rule. A public outcry ensued, and the British government turned the administration of Palestine over to the United Nations. In 1948, the Jewish state of Israel came into existence.

Some scholars maintain that the era of colonialism was in decline and would have come to an end without armed struggle. But Menachem Begin, on the eve of the birth of the nation of Israel, reiterated the view that if he and other terrorists had not taken up arms to fight the British, who enjoyed vast military superiority, the situation would not have changed. "After many years of underground warfare, years of persecution and suffering…[the] Hebrew revolt has been crowned with success," he said. "The rule of enslavement of Britain in our country has been beaten, uprooted, has crumbled and been dispersed. . . . The state of Israel has arisen. And it has arisen 'Only Thus': through blood, fire, and a strong hand and a mighty arm, with suffering and sacrifices."[30]

The Algerian Bloodbath

The terrorism of the Irgun and the even more extreme Stern Gang was carried out with pin-point precision. Only British military and government personnel and facilities were targeted, and during the years of the most intense violence (1945–1947), fewer than 150 British soldiers were killed. Begin and the other terrorists calculated correctly that Britain would respond in a way designed to prevent hostilities from escalating out of control. That

---

A Terrorist Declaration of War

The Algerian National Liberation Front declared a war of terror on the French colonial regime in November 1954 with the following proclamation reprinted online on the Historical Text Archive.

"After decades of struggle, the National Movement has reached its final phase of fulfillment. At home, the people are united behind the watchwords of independence and action. Abroad, the atmosphere is favorable, especially with the diplomatic support of our Arab and Moslem brothers. Our National Movement, prostrated by years of immobility and routine, badly directed, was disintegrating little by little. Faced with this situation, a youthful group, gathering about it the majority of wholesome and resolute elements, judged that the moment had come to take the National Movement out of the impasse into which it had been forced by the conflicts of persons and of influence and to launch it into the true revolutionary struggle. . . . Our movement gives to compatriots of every social position, to all the purely Algerian parties and movements, the possibility of joining in the liberation struggle.

GOAL: National independence through:
1) the restoration of the Algerian state, sovereign, democratic, and social, within the framework of the principles of Islam;
2) the preservation of fundamental freedoms, without distinction of race or religion.

INTERNAL OBJECTIVE: Political housecleaning through the destruction of the last vestiges of corruption and reformism.

EXTERNAL OBJECTIVES:
1) The internationalization of the Algerian problem;
2) The pursuit of North African unity in its national Arabo-Islamic context;
3) The assertion, through United Nations channels, of our active sympathy toward all nations that may support our liberating action.

MEANS OF STRUGGLE: Struggle by every means until our goal is attained. Exertion at home and abroad through political and direct action, with a view to making the Algerian problem a reality for the entire world. The struggle will be long, but the outcome is certain. . . .

Algerians: The F.L.N. is your front; its victory is your victory. For our part, strong in your support, we shall give the best of ourselves to the Fatherland."

restraint was not to be replicated in Algeria when the native population rose up to cast off French colonial rule in 1954. There, the violence spiraled into a bloodbath of terrorism and counterterrorism until revenge and reprisal became ends in themselves. By the time the Algerians won self-rule in 1962, the death toll had reached an estimated 223,000.

France had invaded Algeria in 1830 and made the Muslim North African nation part of its far-flung colonial empire. Almost immediately, Frenchmen began to settle in the area. With the support of the French government and the army, these European colonists, or colons, as they were called, confiscated the best land from the native population and became wealthy farmers, traders, and merchants. Algeria became a divided country, with a European upper class of about 1 million people and a native underclass of about 10 million. The Europeans controlled all aspects of political, economic, and social life, relegating the Algerians to second-class status in their own country. During the nineteenth and early twentieth centuries, there were periodic uprisings against French rule, but these revolts were quickly and brutally put down by the French army. By the end of the Second World War, resentment against French domination was running high.

In 1954, a number of Algerian resistance groups formed a coalition called the National Liberation Front, or FLN (the initials of the organization's French name, Front de Liberation Nationale). On November 1 of that year, they launched a war of independence, issuing a proclamation urging all Algerians to join with them and launching simultaneous terrorist attacks on French government and military installations throughout the country.

For the remainder of 1954, the FLN confined its activities to the countryside, but in August 1955, its leaders instigated a riot in the city of Philippeville. Native Algerians, armed with sticks, axes, and pitchforks, attacked local colons. FLN terrorists threw grenades into cafés and restaurants. For the first time in the twentieth century, terrorists specifically targeted civilians and not just government or military personnel. More than 120 colons died during the violence at Philippeville. French authorities responded with a campaign of counterterror that left, by some accounts, twelve thousand Algerians dead.

Escalating Violence

The terrorism and counterterrorism at Philippeville captured the attention of the world and made the Algerian situation the focus of debate at the United Nations. The FLN became convinced that only through terrorism could it counter the military superiority of the French and keep its cause in the forefront of world opinion. More specifically, FLN leaders concluded that terrorist attacks in cities would get more media coverage than those staged in remote rural areas. Ramdane Abane, the organization's most prominent theoretician, asked, "Is it preferable for our cause to kill ten enemies in an oued [dry riverbed] of Telergma [an obscure country village] when no one will talk of it, or a single man in Algiers [the Algerian capital city] which will be noted the next day by the American press?"[31]

The French authorities began a widespread roundup of suspected terrorists. Every Algerian man became a suspect simply because of his non-European appearance, and thousands of innocent people were detained and tortured. The intense scrutiny made it difficult for FLN operatives to move freely, so the leaders adopted the tactic of using attractive, young, European-looking women to plant bombs. At Abane's insistence, the FLN broadened its range of targets and began sniping at beachgoers, shoppers on the streets of Algiers, tourists at airports—anyone, indeed, who looked like he or she could be a European colonist. Children and the elderly were not spared.

The most devastating attack came when a female FLN operative planted a series of bombs in an Algiers café that was a popular student hangout and a place where colons and their families liked to gather after weekend outings at the seashore. "Exploding only minutes apart, the bombs produced a devastating carnage," writes political scientist Robert Kumamoto. "The glass walls [of the café] shattered into lethal splinters."[32] Three people died, but the flying glass lacerated hundreds of others, many of whom had to have limbs amputated to save their lives. Press photographs of the bloody scene brought about massive retaliation from the French army. In response, the terrorists dispatched death squads to carry out a series of assassinations in France itself.

As the level of terrorist violence increased, the will of the French government to invest more time and manpower into quelling the Algerian revolt began to waver. The colons, fearful that they were about to be abandoned, formed militias and began to slaughter Algerians indiscriminately. The colons also forged an alliance with disaffected military commanders, who then tried to kill French president Charles de Gaulle and take over the government. The attempted coup failed, but it made the French people realize the extent to which the Algerian rebellion, especially the terrorism and counterterrorism it engendered, had infected their lives and eroded the stability of their society.

The attempted assassination of French president Charles de Gaulle signaled a spread of global terrorism.

Legacy of Violence

Seeing that their terrorist activities were beginning to have the desired effect, the FLN stepped up the frequency and intensity of the attacks, against both the colons and Algerians who refused to take part in the struggle. For example, in a bid to eradicate a pocket of pro-colon collaborators in the town of Melouza, FLN commandos rounded up every male older than fifteen, herded them into a mosque, and slaughtered them with rifles and axes.

The colons and their military allies became increasingly desperate and committed a number of atrocities that earned them a reputation for violence equal to that of the insurgents. They freely used torture to glean information about FLN activities, and there were numerous reports of innocent Algerian men and boys being subjected to beatings, electric shocks, and burnings.

Each act of FLN terrorist violence brought an even more extreme response from the colons. In one instance, acting on

Victims of the bloody massacre at Melouza, where FLN commandos slaughtered every male over the age of fifteen.

faulty information that there was a cell of FLN terrorists hiding just across the Algerian border with Tunisia, the colons staged a rocket attack that leveled a school and a hospital, killing hundreds of innocent Tunisians and Algerian refugees. Both sides seemed to forget what they were fighting about and concentrated solely on vengeance for past acts.

Describing this phenomenon, terrorism analyst Martha Crenshaw says,

> Governments or oppositions may initiate terrorism or counter-terrorism as considered responses to the actions of an adversary only to discover they cannot control the process they have set in motion.... In Algeria, violence was often calculated for effect, but these calculations could be motivated by the desire for revenge as much as the desire to produce a change in the behavior of the adversary. Terrorism can become an end in itself. Cruel cycles of retaliatory violence, among Algerians and between Europeans and Algerians, proved impossible to bring to a halt.[33]

Finally, in 1962, the French government admitted that it had lost control of the Algerian situation, and capitulated to FLN demands. Ahmed Ben Bella, an FLN leader, became the first head of the newly independent Algerian state.

Terrorism played a vital role in enabling both Israel and Algeria to throw off the bur-

FLN leader Ahmed Ben Bella became the first leader of independent Algeria.

den of colonial rule and win the right to self-determination. But terrorism also left a legacy of violence that continues to shape the political destinies of the two countries. Israel is under attack from Palestinians, who are using the tactics of terror in an attempt to undermine the Jewish state. Algeria is engulfed in a war of terrorism between its secular government and Arab religious fundamentalists who want to turn the nation into an Islamic republic ruled by religious law. In both cases, analysts admit that there is no end in sight to the bloodshed.

Chapter Four

Terrorism and the Left

Terrorists have been effective in bringing about social and political change when their goals have been specific and they have won the support of the people they claimed to represent. That was so in the case of anticolonial terrorism in the 1940s and '50s. It was clearly not so in the next wave of terrorist activity, the left-wing, anticapitalist violence that swept through Europe and North and South America during the 1960s and '70s. During that period, there was widespread opposition to the war in Vietnam on university campuses around the world. Radical students viewed American involvement in Southeast Asia as an example of imperialism, a form of colonialism in which economic domination, often with military involvement, replaces direct political control of the subjugated nation.

Some of these students concluded that American imperialism was the source of inequality and oppression throughout the world, and that the United States and the countries in Western Europe and South America that supported it had to be totally transformed. A small number of these radicals decided that terrorism was the only way to accomplish that goal. By staging isolated acts of violence, they hoped that they could ignite revolution. But their goal—worldwide revolution—was broad and ill-defined, and the working-class people they were trying to stir up, rather than perceiving themselves to be oppressed, were affluent and enjoyed a high degree of personal freedom. To them, the terrorists appeared to be not liberators or freedom fighters but merely fanatics or criminals.

The Baader-Meinhof Gang

In April 1968, disgruntled former sociology student Andreas Baader and three accomplices set fire to a department store in Frankfurt, West Germany, claiming that in committing the act of terror they were lighting a "torch against the capitalistic terror of consumerism."[34] They were arrested and sentenced to four years in prison. While serving his term, Baader was allowed to collaborate on a book with journalist Ulrike Meinhof, and he converted her to his cause. On May 14, 1970, she helped Baader escape from prison by participating in a daring armed raid during which two guards were shot and wounded. Meinhof left her husband and twin daughters to join with Baader and approxi-

mately sixty followers to form a group called the Red Army Faction (which the press quickly nicknamed Baader-Meinhof Gang.

The gang allied itself with Middle Ea terrorist organizations, sent its members to train at terrorist camps in Jordan, and played a supporting role in the murder of eleven Israeli athletes by the Palestinian Black September commandos at the Munich Olympics in 1972. Also in 1972, they bombed U.S. Army bases in Frankfurt and Hamburg, killing four. Historian David Whittaker has chronicled other Baader-Meinhof acts of terror: "Judges,

Andreas Baader (left) and Ulrike Meinhof formed the Red Army Faction. Both were sentenced to long prison terms and eventually took their own lives.

on governors, and
ambushed and
nd 1977. . . .
.iere had been 108
.ne in three succeeded)
.ings."[35] Baader and Meinhof
.st of these actions from prison;
.ie arrested in 1972 along with a num-
. of other gang members caught in a police
dragnet.

While behind bars, Meinhof organized a hunger strike, which led to the death of her RAF comrade Holger Meins. RAF members still at large blamed the authorities and murdered a judge in retaliation. On April 24, 1975, six RAF commandos shot their way into the West German embassy in Stockholm, Sweden. Says historian Albert Parry, "Seizing hostages, including the Ambassador, they demanded the release of 26 Baader-Meinhof Gang members, among them the two leaders. The [West German] government refused the demand. A shootout with Swedish police followed. The terrorists killed two hostages . . . and tried to escape. All six were captured, one of them mortally wounded in a suicide attempt."[36]

Baader and Meinhof were both sentenced to long prison terms. Without their hands-on guidance, the RAF unraveled under the pressure of effective police measures into a number of splinter groups. In despair that their message of revolution against the influence of American imperialism in Germany had fallen on deaf ears, the two leaders killed themselves in their cells. Although the Baader-Meinhof Gang fell far short of their goal, the massive press coverage their terrorism achieved did cause considerable unease among the German populace. "The effect of German terrorism . . . led to confusion, fear, and even panic until it was seen that the counterterrorism measures of the government were taking hold," Whittaker says. "Taking into account the customary black-and-white, unanalytical style of press reporting, there was real perplexity as to [the Baader-Meinhof Gang's] motivation and future intentions."[37]

The Weather Underground

In the United States, student protest against the war in Vietnam was centered around a radical campus organization known as Students for a Democratic Society (SDS). In 1969, a small faction of the group, dissatisfied with the SDS policy of nonviolence, split to form a terrorist group called the Weather Underground. In a manifesto, the Weather Underground declared, "During the 1960s the American government was on trial for crimes against the people of the world. We now find the government guilty and sentence it to death in the streets. . . . We're going to bring the war home to the mother country of imperialism."[38] At a rally, one of the group's leaders, Bernadine Dohrn, glorified violence when she praised the brutal murders of pregnant actress Sharon Tate and others orchestrated by convicted killer Charles Manson and his followers: "Dig it: first they killed those pigs, then they ate dinner in the same room with them, then they even shoved forks into the victims' stomachs. Wild!"[39]

The members of the Weather Underground organized themselves into small cells around the country and began a bombing campaign against U.S. government facilities

The Black Panthers

The Black Panther Party was founded in 1966 in Oakland, California, by two African American militants, Huey P. Newton and Bobby Seale, who had come to the conclusion that violent revolution was the only way to end racism in America. Newton and Seale called for all African Americans to arm themselves, and party members were involved in a number of shootouts with police. Newton himself was charged with killing a policeman in 1967, but three attempts to convict him of the crime ended in mistrials. Seale was charged, but not convicted, of conspiring to kill a man for informing authorities of the party's plans to stage a number of acts of urban violence. Thirteen Panthers were put on trial in 1971 for conspiring to bomb public facilities in various parts of the country. They, too, were acquitted.

In 1972, Newton and Seale repudiated terrorist tactics. Eldridge Cleaver, the party's media relations officer, continued to advocate violence and fled to Algeria in 1975 to escape prosecution for his role in a shootout. Eventually, Cleaver also softened his stand on the use of violence and returned to America. Although convicted of no crimes, the Panthers were blatant in calling for armed insurrection and advocated terrorist attacks on people and property associated with the economic and political establishment of America.

Urban violence was a frequent subject of discussion in the party's newspaper, the *Black Panther*. The following excerpt is from an article that appeared on April 25, 1970 (reprinted in *The Black Panthers Speak*, edited by Philip Foner). It is an attempt to legitimize terrorism. Like many terrorists before and since, the Panthers justified the use of violence as a form of self-defense against a hostile government. The Panthers portrayed the African American community as a colonized "nation" within the borders of the United States.

> The Black Panther Party recognizes . . . that the only response to the violence of the ruling class is the revolutionary violence of the people. The Black Panther Party recognizes this truth . . . as the basic premise for relating to the colonial oppression of Black People in the heartland of Imperialism where the white ruling class, through its occupation police forces . . . institutionally terrorizes the Black community. Revolutionary strategy for Black people in America begins with the defensive movement of picking up the Gun, as the condition for ending the pigs' reign of terror by the Gun. Black people picking up the Gun for self-defense is the only basis for a revolutionary offensive against Imperialist state power.

and other symbolic targets. Their spectacular acts of terrorism won them much media attention. Especially dramatic were the bombings of the New York City Police Headquarters in June 1970; the Capitol Building in Washington, D.C., in March 1971; and the Pentagon in May 1972. Other targets included banks, prisons, courthouses, universities conducting research for the military, and the head offices of corporations involved in the Vietnam War effort.

Firefighters remove the body of a Weather Underground member killed in a Greenwich Village explosion in March 1970.

Ironically, the Weather Underground's most devastating act of terrorism, the one that caused the most public concern about its potential for destruction, was an accident. On March 6, 1970, an explosion destroyed a high-priced, four-story townhouse in New York City's Greenwich Village. The blast was heard a dozen blocks away and nearby windows were shattered. Amid the rubble, the dismembered bodies of three known Weather Underground operatives were found, and police discovered that they had set up a bomb factory in the building's basement while its owner, a wealthy radio station owner, was on an extended vacation in the Caribbean. The publicity surrounding the event led to a large-scale investigation into the Weather Underground, which resulted in the arrest of several key members and the discovery of plans for additional terrorist acts.

Constant police surveillance hampered the Weather Underground's activities, and the press portrayed them as misguided kids who had turned to terrorism to add adventure to their privileged middle-class lives. The public, whose support the Underground hoped to win, turned on them and demanded that they be rounded up and prosecuted as criminals. Those leaders who had not been arrested went into hiding. Political scientist Ehud Sprinzak describes the movement as a failure:

It never recruited more than 400 members and followers, and most of the time its inexperienced leaders and recruits worried not about the revolution but about their hideouts, survival logistics [strategies], and internal group relations.... Its young leaders never recovered from [the Greenwich Village explosion]; the accident greatly diminished their enthusiasm for terrorism. In their last public document...they admitted that very little had been achieved in the United States.[40]

The Red Brigades

The most successful of the European and North American left-wing terrorist movements was an outgrowth of the Italian student protest movement. Taking their cue from student revolts in other countries, especially France, a group of intellectuals formed the Red Brigades (Brigate Rosse, or BR) in the city of Milan in 1970. The leader was a sociology student named Renato Curcio, and he believed the Red Brigades "would be the vanguard of proletarian resistance against its

---

A Terrorist Manifesto

The Weather Underground announced its program in 1974 in a statement called Prairie Fire, *in which it advanced the unrealistic theory that acts of terrorism would provoke government repression on so vast a scale that the American people would be encouraged to rise in mass revolt. This excerpt of the statement is contained in* The Terrorism Reader, *edited by Walter Laqueur and Yonah Alexander.*

"Armed struggle has come into being in the United States. It is an indication of growth that our movement has developed clandestine organizations and that we are learning how to fight....

At this early stage in the armed and clandestine struggle, our forms of combat and confrontation are few and precise. Our organized forces are small, the enemy's forces are huge. We live inside the oppressor nation, particularly suited to urban guerrilla warfare. We are strategically situated in the nerve centers of the international empire, where the institutions and symbols of imperial power are concentrated. The cities will be a major battleground, for the overwhelming majority of people live in the cities; the cities are our terrain.

We believe that carrying out armed struggle will affect the people's consciousness of the nature of the struggle against the state. By beginning the armed struggle, the awareness of its necessity will be furthered. This is no less true in the U.S. than in other countries throughout the world. Revolutionary action generates revolutionary consciousness; growing consciousness develops revolutionary action. Action teaches the lessons of fighting and demonstrates that armed struggle is possible....

Armed struggle brings the resistance to a sharper and deeper level of development. The greater the resistance, the greater will be the force and scope of state repression brought to bear upon the people. When resistance is at a high level, the enemy takes measures against the people."

fundamental enemy, the Italian incarnation of a 'multinational imperialist state.'. . . . As a means to an end, opponents would have to be marked down and terrorized."[41] In 1970, Italy was in the midst of an economic crisis. Unemployment, especially among the young, was high, and the government was indecisive in responding to the situation. Curcio concluded that the capitalist system was faltering and that the time was ripe for revolution. All that was needed was the spark that terrorism would provide.

Initially, says political scientist Paul Furlong,

> the terrorist attacks mounted by the [Red Brigades] were high in symbolic content and low on physical injury for a considerable period. Arson against cars belonging to managers of large firms . . . with occasional well-planned and well-publicized kidnappings . . . constituted bread-and-butter operations undertaken against representative targets with the aim both of inducing terror among the 'ruling class' and of stimulating the working class to take up arms.[42]

The Red Brigades continued in this fashion until 1972 when, disappointed by the failure of their activities to generate the expected amount of anxiety or support, they escalated their violent attacks to include murder. The Italian police responded by arresting Curcio following a shootout in which the terrorist's wife was killed. The Red Brigades kidnapped Mario Sossi, the assistant attorney general of Genoa, and threatened to execute him if Curcio was not

released. A deal was struck between the government and the terrorists, but Sossi's superior, Francesco Coco, backed out at the last minute. Days later, he was gunned down by Red Brigade assassins.

The Red Brigades were tightly organized. Writing of the years 1974 to 1979, Furlong says,

> The BR now had an articulated organization with established groups— 'columns'—of full-time clandestine terrorists in at least four major cities and probably elsewhere. Each column consists of about six members, one of whom is in touch with the central control; the columns are kept strictly separate from one another. . . . The BR are well-equipped, thorough and determined. . . . They are not short of finance, which they obtain by robbing banks and from kidnapping [for ransom].[43]

The bombings, kidnappings, and murders carried out by the Red Brigades appeared to paralyze the Italian government, which was slow to respond in most instances. Emboldened by this indecisiveness, the terrorists plotted their most daring move, one which would plunge the government into a crisis that many observers thought it would not survive.

On March 16, 1978, Aldo Moro, a leader of the Christian Democrat Party, was being driven by armed security personnel to a church in Rome where he prayed every day before going to his office. As his car approached the church, another vehicle forced it to the side of the street, and Red

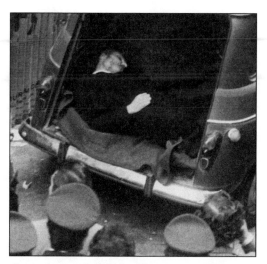

The Red Brigade killed Aldo Moro in 1978, leaving his body in the trunk of a car.

as plumbers kidnapped American general James Dozier, a high-ranking official with NATO (the North Atlantic Treaty Organization), from his apartment in Rome. This time, the United States sent FBI agents to assist the Italian police, and Dozier was freed unharmed. Under pressure from America and other countries, Italian authorities finally initiated a concerted effort to destroy the terrorist organization, and the Red Brigades quickly lost both members and influence. Still, it is estimated that between the years 1970 and 1989, Red Brigade terrorists were responsible for more than two hundred kidnappings and murders.

Brigade terrorists, who had been lying in wait, opened fire with machine guns, killing all five of Moro's bodyguards. They kidnapped the elderly politician and held him for fifty-four days. The saga of Moro's abduction so gripped the public consciousness that no other story appeared on the front page of any Italian newspaper during the time of his captivity. The terrorists demanded the release of the comrades held in jail. The government vacillated. From his confinement, Moro begged the authorities to agree to the terrorists' demands and save his life. His pleas were met with silence. Finally, the terrorists made good on their threat to kill him, and his naked, bullet-riddled body was discovered in the trunk of a car parked on a busy thoroughfare in Rome.

The Red Brigades were so proficient, and the Italian authorities so inept, that they were able to continue their campaign of terror until 1981, when two commandos disguised

The South American Cauldron

Left-wing revolutionary fervor was rife throughout South America during the 1960s and '70s. Fueled by repeated economic crises and consequent high levels of unemployment, radical movements there enjoyed more popular support than did their counterparts in North America and Europe. Also, whereas the European and North American radical organizations had mostly disappeared by the beginning of the 1980s, many such groups in South America continue to be active into the twenty-first century. Terrorism, usually called urban guerrilla warfare by its South American perpetrators, became a commonplace phenomenon in many countries and was typically met with violent government repression.

One of the earliest South American terrorist organizations was the Tupamaros, founded in Uruguay in 1963 by Raul Sendic, a Communist labor organizer. Sendic, who had studied the tactics of guerrilla warfare in Cuba and China, started out by robbing banks. Though he claimed to distribute the stolen money to the poor, he actually used it to purchase weapons for his commandos. By 1968, the Tupamaros were sufficiently well armed to carry out a rash of assassinations, bombings, and kidnappings. They made worldwide headlines in 1970 when they abducted and killed Daniel Mitrione, an American sent by the U.S. government to train Uruguayan police in the methods of counterterrorism.

Other kidnappings and murders followed. Sendic was arrested, but he escaped from prison, underwent plastic surgery to change his appearance, adopted a new identity, and set up a base of operations in the capital city of Montevideo. He was a fearless leader, and his daring exploits made him a cult hero among Uruguay's impoverished workers and peasants. In 1971, for example, he tunneled into a maximum security prison and led 106 Tupamaro prisoners to freedom, later revealing the details to the press to achieve publicity for his cause—transforming Uruguay into a Communist state.

Over time, the Tupamaros became powerful enough to establish a governmental structure that paralleled that of the legal authorities. "The Tupamaros were ruled by a Central Committee and a Secretariat," says Albert Parry. "The rank and file were divided into 'columns,' with strict delineation of specialties and duties. For instance, a well-meshed sector of men and women ran 'people's prisons' where the kidnapped were kept. An International Affairs Committee took care

of cooperation with terrorist groups outside Uruguay."[44]

Repression

By 1972, the Tupamaros felt powerful enough to attack the Uruguayan army directly. It was a costly mistake. The government, under President Juan Maria Bordaberry, officially declared war on the terrorists, suspending civil liberties, closing down newspapers and the country's only university, and detaining thousands of suspected Tupamaro sympathizers without trial. The army and police blatantly used torture to glean information on the terrorists' organization and activities,

Uruguayan president Juan Maria Bordaberry tried to stop the left-wing terrorist network Tupamaro.

driving the Tupamaros underground. One victim of torture cracked and led police to an apartment in Montevideo where Sendic and his girlfriend were hiding. The leader was seriously wounded in a shootout and taken into custody.

The Tupamaros fought back with a torrent of frenzied violence. In a two-month period, they carried out eight kidnappings, thirty-five armed attacks on police stations, and sixty assaults on office buildings and private homes. They killed fifteen people, wounded dozens more, and caused millions of dollars in property damage. The government responded by expanding their repressive measures, suspending both houses of the Uruguayan congress. The power of the army increased, and the president became little more than a figurehead, effectively putting an end to democracy in Uruguay. The repressive measures put an end to the Tupamaro terrorism. Most of the organization's leadership was jailed; the rest abandoned the struggle and either fled the country or melted back into the general population.

A similar fate awaited South America's other terrorist movements—among them the National Liberation Action and the People's Revolutionary Vanguard in Brazil, the People's Revolutionary Army and the Montoneros in Argentina, the National Liberation Army in Bolivia, the Left Revolutionary Movement in Chile, and the Revolutionary Armed Forces in Colombia. Left-wing terrorism provoked right-wing repression and counterterrorism, often leading to military dictatorship.

In many countries, the struggle continues. For example, in 1997, the Shining Path in Peru conducted more than 450 terrorist operations resulting in 100 deaths. In some cases, the terrorists have abandoned their political operations but not the violence with which they carried them out. These have become roaming mobs of bandits, extorting money from terrified farmers in rural areas and, in Colombia especially, forming alliances with drug cartels, providing the cocaine manufacturers with protection from government interference in their illegal operations.

Chapter Five

Separatist Terrorism

As the left-wing social revolutionary terrorism of the 1960s and '70s was reaching its full level of intensity, nationalism emerged as an additional motive for political violence among two peoples, the Irish and the Basques. In these cases, the desire that drove men and women to take up arms was not the transformation of society into a socialist utopia; rather, their goal was the creation of separate states where they felt they could establish institutions that would fully express their unique ethnic and religious collective personalities. The Irish Roman Catholics who inhabited the six counties that make up Northern Ireland, or Ulster, felt trapped within Great Britain. The Basques, on the other hand, lived in the area that falls on either side of the border dividing France and Spain. The Irish Catholics and the Basques each wanted their own nation, and each was prepared to shed blood to get it.

"Bloody Sunday"

The roots of what has come to be called the Irish Troubles go back to the early sixteenth century, when England, a Protestant country, tried to cement its authority over the Roman Catholic island off its west coast by giving large parcels of Irish land to Protestant settlers from Scotland. The policy caused great resentment in Ireland and brought about periodic armed uprisings that lasted into the twentieth century. In the 1860s, one of these revolts was led by a group that called itself the Irish Republican Army (IRA). In 1949, after much political wrangling and violence, the southern, predominantly Catholic, part of Ireland attained the status of an independent nation. The six northernmost counties, mostly Protestant, remained a province of Great Britain.

The story of the struggle for Irish independence may have ended at that point were it not for the fact that Roman Catholics formed a significant minority in the six northern counties. They had opposed the partition of the island into northern and southern halves, fearing they would become second-class citizens in Ulster and suffer discrimination at the hands of the Protestant majority. Their concerns were justified. In the 1960s, inspired by the civil rights movement in the United States, the Catholics began to campaign for better employment opportunities and better housing. The IRA,

Crisis in Quebec

The separatist terrorism that has claimed so many lives in Ireland and the Basque country also occurred in the early 1960s in the French-speaking Canadian province of Quebec. The Quebec Liberation Front (or FLQ, the initials of the group's French name, Front de Liberation du Quebec) came into existence in 1961 amid rising sentiment among Quebec intellectuals that the province should separate from English-speaking Canada and develop its own culture and political and economic institutions. The majority favored a peaceful, negotiated disengagement from Canada, but a very small group of impatient radicals turned to terrorism in an attempt to speed the process. Between 1961 and 1970, the FLQ conducted a series of sporadic bombings, targeting military and federal government facilities. They also planted bombs in mailboxes in a wealthy English-speaking enclave in Montreal and sent letter bombs to a number of English-owned businesses. There were several casualties, but the government acted with restraint.

Unhappy that their actions appeared to be having little effect on public opinion, the FLQ decided to adopt more dramatic tactics. In October 1970, two 12-man terrorist cells kidnapped the British trade commissioner James Cross and the Quebec minister of labor Pierre Laporte. Robert Bourassa, the premier of Quebec, fearing that he was in mortal danger, fled into hiding. Believing the kidnappings were the beginning of a wholesale insurrection, the federal government, under Prime Minister Pierre Trudeau, invoked the War Measures Act, suspending many civil liberties, and sent the army into Quebec to maintain order. The terrorists issued two demands: that a manifesto calling for Quebec's secession from Canada be published and that imprisoned FLQ members be released. The government agreed to the first demand but balked at the second. Cross was eventually released, but the cell holding Laporte chose to murder him. His body was found in the trunk of a taxi parked in downtown Montreal.

Laporte's killers were brought to trial and sentenced to lengthy jail terms. The government crackdown brought about by the kidnappings resulted in the arrest of many other FLQ members and supporters, effectively putting an end to the movement. Quebec eventually elected a pro-separatist government, but the population declined to ratify separation in a subsequent referendum. The subject of the province's secession from Canada remains a matter of intense national debate.

which had continued to exist as an underground organization, was divided on whether or not to support the Northern Catholics in their struggle for equal opportunity. In 1969, the IRA split, and members sympathetic to the plight of the Catholics in the North formed a new group called the Provisional IRA (Provos).

Violence erupted on January 30, 1972, when Northern Irish Catholics staged a peaceful Sunday protest march in the city of Londonderry. Their parade route was lined with hostile Protestants. Insults were exchanged, rocks flew, and British soldiers, on hand to maintain order, fired into the crowd, killing thirteen Catholic marchers. The incident became known as Bloody Sunday, and it galvanized the Provos into action. Declaring themselves the defenders of the Catholic community in Northern Ireland, the group embarked on a war of terror against the British and the Protestant majority. Their weapon of choice was the car bomb—a car loaded with explosives set to detonate when it would cause the most destruction and garner the most publicity. Their preferred targets were public places, pubs, or bars, and shopping districts patronized by Protestants, as well as British military and governmental organizations.

An armed soldier attacks a protester on Bloody Sunday. That day's events detonated an era of terrorist violence in Northern Ireland.

Ireland: A Protestant Perspective

In the 1970s, the Protestant community in Northern Ireland felt that the British government was not doing enough to protect them from terrorist violence, especially since their enemy, the Irish Republican Army, was receiving technical assistance from the Soviet Union and financial support from sympathizers in the United States. The Protestants' desperation and sense of abandonment is expressed in this anonymous letter printed in the Dublin Sunday World *newspaper on June 9, 1973.*

"Traditionally the English politicians let us down—betrayal we call it. The Catholics try to overwhelm us so we are caught between two lines of fire. Second-class Englishmen, half-caste Irishmen, this we can live with and even defeat it, but how can we be expected to beat the world revolutionary movement which supplies arms and training, not to mention most sophisticated advice on publicity, promotion, and expertise to the IRA?

We do not have large funds from over-indulgent sentimentally sick Irishmen in America who send the funds of capitalism to sow the seeds of communism here.... We are betrayed and maligned, and our families live in constant fear and misery. We are a nuisance to our so-called allies and have no friends anywhere. Once more in the history of our people we have our backs to the wall, facing extinction by one way or another. This is the moment to beware, for Ulstermen in this position fight mercilessly till they or their enemies are dead."

Provo terrorism was both indiscriminate—many innocent civilians were killed in their attacks—and, in the opinion of terrorism expert Walter Laqueur, exceptionally inhumane. The terror, Laqueur stated in 2001,

was not directed against the leadership of the enemy camp; but, on the other hand, bars, stores, and public transport were among the favorite aims of bomb attacks.... What distinguishes the most recent phase of Irish terrorism from all previous outbreaks is [its]…almost pathological cruelty, which was not in the tradition of even the most extreme Irish freedom fighters of past generations."[45]

The British responded to Provo terrorism with a program of internment, in which suspects were rounded up and imprisoned without trial.

Bombings and Assassinations

The Provos took their terrorism into England itself, bombing pubs in several cities and the famous Harrods department store in London, among hundreds of other targets. They assassinated Lord Louis Mountbatten, a British World War II hero and uncle of heir to the throne Prince Charles, and eighteen soldiers on the same day in coordinated attacks. They also attempted to kill British prime minister Margaret Thatcher by placing a bomb under her chair at a political rally in the city of

Masked members of the IRA bear the coffin of outspoken Provo Bobby Sands, who died during a hunger strike in 1981.

Birmingham in 1984. When the explosive failed to detonate due to a faulty computer chip in its timer, the Provos issued a warning to Thatcher and other politicians that future attacks would take place. "Today we were unlucky," they said in a statement released to the press, "but remember we only have to be lucky once—you will have to be lucky always."[46] The Provos came close to wiping out the entire cabinet of Thatcher's successor, John Major, in 1991 when a remote control rocket attack narrowly missed his official residence at 10 Downing Street in London.

The British policy of internment caused jails to fill with Provos and their sympathizers, who insisted on being treated as political prisoners. When this demand was rejected, the inmates staged a hunger strike. Thirteen of them, including Bobby Sands, an outspoken Provo who had been elected to a seat in the British Parliament, starved to death amid massive media coverage that generated an enormous amount of support for the terrorists among Northern Ireland's Catholic population. Provo terrorism provoked a violent response from Northern Ireland's Protestant majority, who formed their own terrorist organizations. These groups committed a series of bombings and assassinations in retaliation for Provo violence and once paralyzed all of Northern Ireland for a day when they sabotaged water supplies across the province.

The scope of terrorist violence in Northern Ireland, and the amount of social and economic disruption it has caused, is virtually unprecedented in the history of political violence. The disorder, reported the *Belfast Telegraph* newspaper in 1997, "led to the greatest population movement in western Europe since World War II as thousands of families fled from mixed [Catholic and Protestant] areas. In Belfast [the capital of Northern Ireland] entire streets of homes were torched as mobs went on the rampage and in Londonderry the police were almost overwhelmed.... During the Troubles, security forces logged some 35,000 shooting incidents and 10,000 explosions."[47]

There have been repeated attempts to negotiate a peaceful resolution to the conflict in Northern Ireland, but finding a way to satisfy both sides has so far proved to be impossible. Every time progress is made, as with an agreement in 1997 to disarm both Catholic and Protestant terrorist groups, dissidents from one camp or the other perpetrate an act of violence to derail the peace process. After one such attack, the *Belfast Telegraph* pessimistically reported that the "violence had not gone away—and possibly never would."[48]

Basque Terrorism

The Basques are an ancient people who inhabit the mountainous region covering the north of Spain and the south of France. They have their own language, called Euskera, which is not related to any other European tongue. They also have a distinct culture, which is neither Spanish nor French, yet they have not had a separate homeland since the

year 1035. Until the twentieth century, they were allowed to exist relatively undisturbed, mostly in Spain (approximately 2.5 million Basques live in Spain, while another 500,000 live in France). However, when General Francisco Franco seized power in Spain in 1939, his dictatorial government set out to suppress minorities within the country. He outlawed the Basque language and tried through force to integrate the Basques into Spanish society.

"The Francoist regime engaged in physical and symbolic repression of any outward manifestation of Basque cultural and political identity," say political scientists Goldie

Spanish dictator Francisco Franco tried to force the Basques to integrate into Spanish society.

Shabad and F. J. L. Ramos. "As a result, Basques ... came to view their territory as suffering 'military occupation' by an illegitimate Spanish state."[49] In the 1950s, Basque intellectuals formed the Basque Nationalist Party, which sought—through peaceful means—to pressure the government into a more lenient position on the issue of self-determination. A group of impatient young Nationalist Party members, dissatisfied with the lack of progress, formed a terrorist organization called Basque Homeland and Liberty (Euskadi Ta Askatasuna, or ETA) in 1958.

A year later, the ETA carried out its first military operations, bombings in the cities of Bilba, Vitoria, and Santander. In 1962, the group bungled an attempt to derail a train carrying Spanish war veterans to a celebration. Because the attack targeted people regarded as war heroes, there was a public outcry, and police rounded up and jailed many ETA terrorists. The authorities used torture to compel prisoners to reveal the names of their associates, and hundreds of ETA members and supporters went into exile to escape arrest.

A hard-core ETA faction remained in Spain and stepped up the campaign of terror. Their most spectacular act was the assassination in 1973 of Admiral Luis Carrero Blanco, the Spanish premier and heir-apparent to the aging Franco. Four ETA operatives rented a ground-floor apartment in Madrid on the street along which Blanco traveled every morning to church services. Pretending to be sculptors to provide themselves with an excuse for the noise, they dug a tunnel under the road, planted 165 pounds of dynamite and plastic explosives, and ran an electrical wire from a detonator back to the apartment. On the morning of December 20, they parked a car on the street in such a way that Blanco's driver would have to steer his vehicle directly over the massive bomb. At 9:30 A.M., as the admiral's car reached the exact spot they anticipated it would, the terrorists triggered their bomb. Historian Albert Parry describes the devastation: "The Premier's vehicle was hurled upward with tremendous force, over the roof of five stories, and landed on the terrace surrounding the inner patio of the church. The Premier was dying in the wreckage."[50]

Intimidation and Vengeance

Historians have argued that in killing Blanco, the ETA effectively brought down the Franco regime. When the dictator died in 1976, there was no one to replace him. The absence of a successor allowed the Spanish people to elect a democratic government, which granted the Basque region its own parliament and control of its education system, and guaranteed that the distinctive Basque language could be taught in state-funded schools. This partial autonomy satisfied the majority of the Basques, but not the ETA, whose operatives had returned from exile once Franco's police state was abolished. They insisted that the Basque lands become fully independent of Spain, and resumed their interrupted war of terror.

Although the ETA had no more than twenty hard-core terrorists (by some estimates) and only several hundred active supporters, the members accumulated money

Wreckage from the blast that killed Spanish premier Luis Carrero Blanco in 1973.

to buy sophisticated weapons through bank robberies, kidnap ransoms, and drug trafficking. They also used the threat of violence to terrorize the Basque population itself into paying them what they referred to as a revolutionary tax. The ETA became experts at political assassination, by both gun and bomb, focusing their terrorist efforts principally on Spanish politicians and government officials, the police and military, and judges and prosecutors. They also committed acts of terrorism in France in response to attempts by French authorities to hinder the activities of ETA members living there.

The ETA has also carried its terrorism into the Basque community, vengefully killing those it feels are unsympathetic to its radical agenda and intimidating the populace into a silent acceptance of the violence. "Most killings occur in broad daylight in the streets," says political scientist Jose Trevino.

On other occasions the terrorists calmly walk into a bar or cafeteria.... Often without even bothering to conceal their identities, the terrorists single out their targets and 'execute' them in front of scores of onlookers. Yet, when police investigators try to ascertain the facts, witnesses are almost impossible to find. ... The fear of associating or collaborating with the police is well founded. There is little doubt that the ETA has an effective intelligence network which pervades almost every segment of Basque society.[51]

Spanish authorities estimate that the ETA has carried out more than one hundred assassinations and forty-six kidnappings, for which they were paid millions of dollars in ransom. The high-profile status of the victims keeps the group constantly in the news. Early in its history, the ETA chose to organize itself into a small number of cells that operate independently of each other, making it difficult for Spanish police to infiltrate the organization and disrupt its activities. The ETA has also forged links with a number of other terrorist organizations around the world. Its operatives have trained in Libya, Lebanon, and Nicaragua. Through its political wing, it is in regular contact with the Irish Republican Army.

Self-Perpetuating Violence

The Spanish government, although initially receptive to Basque demands for more autonomy, has hardened its stance in response to

The ETA, responsible for this car bombing, is organized into independent cells that help members elude Spanish police.

the ETA's unceasing terrorist activity. In 1997, all twenty-seven members of the organization's political and publicity wing were arrested and sentenced to seven-year prison terms for maintaining ties with the terrorist branch. That same year, more than 6 million people across Spain took to the streets to protest ETA terrorism after the group brutally murdered a young Basque boy they suspected of collaborating with authorities.

In 1998, the ETA agreed to a cease-fire as a prelude to negotiations, but the truce quickly broke down. The government accused the ETA of using the cease-fire as a stalling tactic so that they could replenish their supply of arms, implicating the terrorists in a series of raids on arms depots. During the cease-fire, the ETA did not conduct any assassinations, but members continued to carry out attacks on property belonging to the government and its officials.

In November 1999, the ETA announced that it had officially ended the cease-fire, blaming government repression and the unwillingness of more moderate Basque politicians to push for a fully independent state. The terrorists resumed their campaign of assassination, rocking Spanish society with a series of shootings and car bombings.

On July 15, 2001, the people of Spain once again staged a protest. The demonstrations resulted from the ETA's assassination of conservative politician Jose Javier Mugica Astibia, who was killed by a bomb, and the slaying of Mikel Urbe, the police chief of the Basque town of Hernani, who was shot to death by two assailants in a park.

Analysts pessimistically predict that terrorism will continue to infect Basque soci-

Protesters shout slogans condemning the terrorist actions of the ETA.

ety—and Irish society as well. In both cases, they argue, violence has produced a class of professional terrorists who know no other way to conduct their lives.

> The parallels between the IRA and the Basque ETA are striking in many respects," says Walter Laqueur. "Both are motivated by enormous enthusiasm, even though the groups constitute only a minority within their own community. ... In the Basque region, as in Northern Ireland, a culture of violence has developed over the years that tends to perpetuate itself. It is in all probability a generational question. As one generation of professional terrorists ages and by necessity opts out of the armed struggle, a new one emerges.[52]

Chapter Six

Holy War

As left-wing furor flared in Europe and the Americas, and separatist rage created a climate of fear in Ireland and the Basque country, a new form of terrorism emerged in the Middle East. This brand of political violence, that has come to be called Islamic terrorism, would come to dominate world headlines for the rest of the century. It also added two particularly potent and grisly tactics to the terrorist arsenal: airplane hijackings and suicide bombings.

Islamic terrorism falls into two categories. The first, exemplified by the Palestine Liberation Organization (PLO) and groups affiliated with it, is secular, or nonreligious, in nature; its goal is the creation of an independent Palestinian state within the territory now occupied by Israel. The second type of Islamic terrorism, embodied in organizations such as Hamas,

Hizballah, the Islamic Jihad, and al-Qaeda, is inspired by a fierce, uncompromising Islamic fundamentalism, and its goal is to spread the Muslim faith throughout the world. Between the late 1960s and the 1990s, dozens of groups sprang into existence. At times they cooperated with each other; at other times they feuded; to confuse their enemies, they frequently changed their names, and their members drifted from one organization to another. Further complicating an already confusing picture, the governments of three nations—Iran, Iraq, and Libya—employed these terrorists to advance their international political agendas by violent means.

The Problem of Israel

Common to all Islamic terrorism is opposition to the existence of the Jewish state of Israel in the midst of land that Muslims regard as given to them by God. Albert Parry refers to this dedication to the destruction of Israel as "the world's bloodiest terror."[53] The first Islamic terrorist organization to take up arms against the state of Israel was the PLO, founded in 1964 to forge a united front to fight for Palestine's return to Arab rule. Among the terrorist groups that joined the PLO was Fatah, headed by Yasir Arafat. Arafat used his political cunning to take over the organization and become its chairman in 1967.

At first, Arafat was blatant in calling for the Jews to be driven out of the Middle East, and adopted a terrorist strategy to achieve that end. But he also realized the importance of establishing the PLO as a legitimate voice for the Palestinian people in the international community. Thus, he attempted to disguise the organization's involvement in terrorist activity by using other groups to carry out the actions. In 1970, for example, the PLO used a cover group called Black September, an offshoot of the Popular Front for the Liberation of Palestine (PFLP), to stage the

Yasir Arafat, leader of the Palestine Liberation Organization, called for the Jews to be driven out of the Middle East. He has since softened his position.

simultaneous hijacking of four airliners. Three of the hijackings succeeded, and the planes were flown to Jordan and Cairo, where they were destroyed after the passengers were taken off.

The fourth hijack attempt failed. One of the terrorists was killed and the other, a woman Black September commando named Leila Khaled, was wounded and taken into custody by British authorities after the plane landed at Heathrow airport in London, England. Khaled's capture caused an international crisis. The PFLP demanded her release and threatened to kill the passengers on the other hijacked planes, sixty-five of whom were citizens of England, if the British did not comply.

Black September commando Leila Khaled brandishes a machine gun.

Britain had signed an agreement, along with Israel, the United States, and other countries, promising not to negotiate with hijackers under any circumstances. But with sixty-five British lives at stake, the government of Prime Minister Edward Heath wavered and gave in to the terrorists' demands, releasing Khaled. Israel and the United States were furious, fearing that Britain's capitulation would encourage other terrorist acts. The episode was regarded by the PFLP as a major victory. Speaking of the incident thirty-one years later to an interviewer from the British Broadcasting Corporation, Khaled said, "It was a good step for us that we saw governments could be negotiated with.... The success in the tactics of the hijacking and imposing our demands and succeeding in having our demands implemented gave us the courage and the confidence to go ahead with our struggle."[54]

Massacre at Munich

Another Black September operation proved that terrorism could succeed in attracting publicity even if the specific act failed. To bring the cause of Palestinian independence to the world's attention, eight Black September terrorists burst into a dormitory housing eleven Israeli athletes at the 1972 Olympic Games in Munich, Germany. Two athletes were killed in the initial attack; the nine others were taken hostage. The terrorists demanded the release of 236 Palestinians from Israeli jails, five other terrorists (including Andreas Baader and Ulrike Meinhof, the leaders of the Baader-Meinhof Gang) held in Germany, and safe passage back to the Middle East.

Palestinian Declaration of Independence

On November 15, 1988, the Palestine Liberation Organization issued a declaration of independence on behalf of the Arab population of Palestine. In this excerpt, from the Palestinian National Authority website, the PLO looks back on the violence that has characterized the recent history of the Middle East. Typical of groups that have been labeled terrorist, they refer to themselves as liberation fighters and to their enemies as the real terrorists.

"In the name of God, the Compassionate, the Merciful...

Resolute throughout that history, the Palestinian Arab people forged its national identity, rising even to unimagined levels in its defense, as invasion, the design of others... intervened thereby to deprive the people of its political independence. Yet the undying connection between Palestine and its people secured for the land its character, and for the people its national genius....

In generation after generation, the Palestinian Arab people gave of itself unsparingly in the valiant battle for liberation and homeland. For what has been the unbroken chain of our people's rebellions but the heroic embodiment of our will for national independence. And so the people was sustained in the struggle to stay and to prevail.

When in the course of modern times a new order of values was declared with norms and values fair for all, it was the Palestinian Arab people that had been excluded from the destiny of all other peoples by a hostile array of local and foreign powers. Yet again had unaided justice been revealed as insufficient to drive the world's history along its preferred course....

By stages, the occupation of Palestine and parts of other Arab territories by Israeli forces, the willed dispossession and expulsion from their ancestral homes of the majority of Palestine's civilian inhabitants, was achieved by organized terror; those Palestinians who remained, as a vestige subjugated in its homeland, were persecuted and forced to endure the destruction of their national life....

Occupation, massacres and dispersion achieved no gain in the unabated Palestinian consciousness of self and political identity, as Palestinians went forward with their destiny, undeterred and unbowed. And from out of the long years of trial in ever-mounting struggle, the Palestinian political identity emerged further consolidated and confirmed. And the collective Palestinian national will forged for itself a political embodiment, the Palestine Liberation Organization, its sole, legitimate representative.... The PLO led the campaigns of its great people, molded into unity and powerful resolve, one and indivisible in its triumphs, even as it suffered massacres and confinement within and without its home. And so Palestinian resistance was clarified and raised into the forefront of Arab and world awareness, as the struggle of the Palestinian Arab people achieved unique prominence among the world's liberation movements in the modern era....

Now by virtue of natural, historical and legal rights, and the sacrifices of successive generations who gave of themselves in defense of the freedom and independence of their homeland ... the Palestine National Council, in the name of God, and in the name of the Palestinian Arab people, hereby proclaims the establishment of the State of Palestine on our Palestinian territory with its capital Jerusalem."

Masked Black Septembrists invade Munich's Olympic Village in 1972. Members of the group killed nine Israeli athletes.

The events unfolded in front of the world's media, which had gathered in Munich to cover the Olympics. After fifteen hours of tense negotiations, a settlement appeared to have been reached and the terrorists and their hostages were transported by helicopter to an airfield. As four of the terrorists emerged to inspect the jetliner that was to fly them to freedom, five German police sharpshooters opened fire. The terrorists still on the helicopters fought back with guns and grenades. They also started murdering the hostages they were holding. The carnage, televised live into hundreds of millions of homes around the world, ended with all nine Israeli athletes, five Black Septembrists, and one policeman dead. The three surviving terrorists were taken into custody.

"Both operations—the hostage seizure and the rescue attempt—were colossal failures," says terrorism expert Bruce Hoffman. "The grisly denouement [ending] on the airfield tarmac, broadcast via television and radio throughout the world, was initially regarded as disastrous to the Palestinian cause: a stunning failure and a grave miscalculation, generating revulsion rather than sympathy and condemnation instead of support."[55] In the face of overwhelming evidence that the PLO was involved in the attack, Arafat continued to protest his innocence through a series of speeches and interviews, capitalizing on the publicity generated by the Munich massacre and using the media attention it provided as an opportunity to relentlessly argue the justice of the Palestinian cause.

The strategy worked. Two years later, over the bitter objections of Israel and its steadfast ally the United States, the PLO was granted observer status at the United Nations, allowing it to take part in discussions but not to vote. Arafat was invited to address the world body in 1974, and he was treated with the same dignity accorded to heads of state. "The Olympic tragedy provided the first clear evidence that even terrorist attacks which fail to achieve their ostensible objectives can nonetheless still be counted successful provided that the operation is sufficiently dramatic to capture the media's attention," Hoffman says. "In terms of the publicity and exposure accorded to the Palestinian cause, Munich was an unequivocal success."[56]

Throughout the 1980s and '90s, Arafat distanced the PLO from terrorist activity, although the Israeli government has provided compelling evidence that he continued to use affiliated organizations like the Popular Front for the Liberation of Palestine to carry out acts of violence against both Israel and the United States. For example, in 2001, the PFLP was implicated in eleven car bombings. Yet, as a result of Arafat's skill-ful manipulation of public opinion (he claims the PFLP is beyond his control), the PLO has come to be regarded as the legitimate representative of the Palestinian people. Arafat entered into a series of negotiations with various Israeli prime ministers in an attempt to forge a way in which Jews and Arabs can peacefully coexist in Palestine. These efforts have met with only limited success, and terrorist violence—and Israeli retaliation—continues to hinder the peace process.

Jihad

At the same time that Arafat was apparently trying to move the PLO away from terrorism, the entire Islamic world was undergoing a profound change. In country after country, movements arose that advocated a militant, fundamentalist interpretation of Muslim scripture. The religious leadership of these movements condemned what they saw as the corruption of Islam by Western culture; they also called for the transformation of existing states into Islamic republics, to be governed by mullahs (clerics) in accordance with principles laid down in the Muslim holy book, the Koran. The militants cited certain passages from the Koran as dictating that it was the moral and religious obligation of every Muslim to wage a holy war, or jihad, to erase all traces of non-Muslim influence from the Arab world.

In 1979, one such movement, led by Ayatollah Ruhollah Khomeini, established an Islamic republic in Iran. Khomeini immediately announced his intention: "We must strive to export our Revolution throughout the world."[57] The ayatollah dispatched Iranian agents to Lebanon, where, in 1982, they helped to establish a terrorist organization called Hizballah (Party of God). In a statement released three years later, Hizballah declared its political objectives. "The Hizballah organization views as an important goal the fight against 'western imperialism' and its eradication from Lebanon," the document said. "The conflict with Israel is viewed as a central concern. . . . The complete destruction of the State of Israel and the establishment of Islamic rule over Jerusalem is an expressed goal."[58]

Hizballah committed scores of terrorists acts against Israel, but it also targeted the American presence in Lebanon, hoping to undermine the U.S. support for the Jewish state. On April 18, 1983, a Hizballah suicide terrorist drove a truck containing two thousand pounds of explosives into the American embassy in Beirut, the Lebanese capital city. The blast tore off the front part of the seven-story building and killed 63 people, including 17 Americans. In another suicide bombing six months later, 241 sleeping U.S. Marines were killed when a terrorist drove an explosives-filled truck into a Beirut barracks. The following year,

Cranes remove rubble from the crumbling remains of the American embassy in Beirut, Lebanon after a truck bomb exploded, killing sixty-three people.

a similar attack claimed 24 American lives at the U.S. Embassy Annex, also in Beirut.

The Americans eventually withdrew their forces from Lebanon, but remained supportive of Israel. Hizballah has vowed to continue its campaign of suicide terror until Israel is destroyed and American influence in the Arab world is obliterated. The organization's spiritual leader, Sheik Muhammed Husayn Fadlallah defends suicide bombing as a way of combating overwhelming military might:

> If an oppressed people does not have the means to confront the United States and Israel with the weapons in which they are superior…they must fight with special means of their own. [We] recognize the right of nations to use every unconventional method to fight these aggressor nations, and do not regard what oppressed Muslims of the world do with primitive and unconventional means to confront aggressor powers as terrorism. We view this as religiously lawful warfare against the world's imperialist and domineering powers.[59]

"Combat Between Good and Evil"

The faltering attempts by the Israelis and the PLO to find a way to live together in harmony have been hampered by another terrorist organization whose chosen method of attack is the suicide bombing. Hamas (an Arabic word denoting courage or bravery), also known as the Islamic Resistance Movement, was founded in 1978 by Sheik Ahmed Yassin. Like the PLO, Hamas believes

Ahmed Yassin founded the Hamas terrorist organization, which calls for an Islamic republic for Palestinians.

that the Palestinians should have their own independent state. However, Hamas wants that state to be an Islamic republic, ruled not by elected representatives of the Palestinian people but by Muslim clerics. Therefore, the leaders of Hamas regard both Israel and the PLO as their enemies and have employed terrorism against both.

Hamas is particularly concerned that the Israelis and the PLO will reach an agreement that will allow a secular Palestinian state to be established in the Middle East. Whenever the two sides appear to be nearing such a settlement, Hamas launches a wave of terrorist attacks in the hope that Israeli reprisals will alienate Palestinian supporters of the PLO. Analysts of Middle East affairs admit that the tactic has met with a large degree of success, particularly in the 1990s. "Hamas stepped up its attacks in 1995 and 1996, partly because it wanted to show that it was the leading—indeed the only—militant force now that the PLO had abandoned terrorism for its new respectability," says historian Walter Laqueur. "The peace process seemed to be in full swing, and Hamas tried to sabotage it through a series of massive attacks."[60]

Whereas Hizballah favored suicide truck and car bombings, Hamas chose to have its suicide bombers strap explosives to their bodies and mingle with crowds in marketplaces or on public transportation before detonating the devices. This they were able to do thanks to the efforts of an engineer named Yehya Ayash, who was adept at creating miniature, easily concealed bombs. Ayash became the victim of his own tactics in 1996, when Israeli undercover counterterrorist forces planted a tiny bomb in his cell phone and set it off by remote control while he was talking to his father.

Hamas recruits its suicide bombers from among young Palestinians, who have been indoctrinated to believe that martyrdom in the cause of the jihad against Israel and secular influences in general will guarantee them a place in paradise. The organization has been implicated in more than one hundred suicide bombings since 1989. Its activities have occasioned severe reprisals on the part of the Israelis. These attacks have been directed not only at Hamas but

at the Palestinian population in general, who, the Israelis charge, provide Hamas operatives with support.

The members of Hamas, along with other religion-inspired terrorists, view the struggle they are engaged in as more than political. Rather, they see it in cosmic terms: Sheik Yassin calls it "the combat between good and evil"[61] in which there can be no compromise. Unlike the PLO, which is prepared to make concessions to Israel in the interest of reaching a settlement, Hamas and other like-minded groups have vowed to continue their terrorist struggle until all non-Islamic elements are driven from the Middle East.

Al-Qaeda and the Future of Terrorism

The history of terrorism took a sharp and ominous turn on September 11, 2001. Prior to that date, terrorist attacks, though often devastating in psychological terms, had been somewhat limited in scope. Victims were usually numbered in single or double digits, very rarely exceeding one hundred. But on September 11, in a tightly coordinated and meticulously planned plot, nineteen terrorists belonging to a group called al-Qaeda hijacked four jet airliners from Boston's Logan Airport, cut the throats of the pilots and copilots, and flew two of the planes into the twin towers of New York's World Trade Center and one into the Pentagon building in Washington, D.C. The fourth plane, headed for another, unspecified building in Washington, crashed in a Pennsylvania field after passengers overpowered the hijackers. The planes that reached their targets had, in effect, been turned into flying bombs, causing unprecedented destruction and killing approximately four thousand innocent victims.

The organization responsible, al-Qaeda, had built a network of operatives in an estimated sixty-three countries. It was masterminded by a wealthy Saudi Arabian named Osama bin Laden who had turned his back on a life of luxury to fight his own Islamic holy war against America, a country he had often referred to as the Great Satan. In bin Laden's mind, America's powerful interna-

Al-Qaeda ringleader Osama bin Laden.

tional economy had corrupted the Muslim world and had to be destroyed. He was convinced this was an attainable goal because he had helped the Afghan people defeat the world's other great superpower, the Soviet Union, in the 1980s. Bin Laden believed that a small group of dedicated holy warriors, prepared to sacrifice their lives in the struggle, could bring America to its knees.

To this end, he invested his considerable fortune into building al-Qaeda, an international alliance of Muslim extremists forged into a united whole by sophisticated communications technology. Prior to September 11, al-Qaeda operatives had been responsible for blowing up American embassies in the African countries of Kenya and Tanzania on August 7, 1998, killing 254 and injuring 5,000. Al-Qaeda had also been implicated in a previous truck bomb attack on the World Trade Center in 1993 and in attempts to assassinate Pope John Paul II and Egyptian president Hosni Mubarak. The September 11 attacks prompted U.S. president George W. Bush to take the unprecedented step of declaring a worldwide war on terrorism. He sent American troops into Afghanistan to destroy al-Qaeda bases located there.

Although U.S. efforts disrupted al-Qaeda operations, the network remained largely intact as of February 2002. While searching for evidence in the organization's Afghan camps, intelligence officers discovered a document titled *Manual of Afghan Jihad*, which contained a blueprint for future attacks on America and its allies. "There must be plans for hitting buildings with high human intensity like skyscrapers, ports, airports, nuclear power plants and places where large numbers of people gather," the document said. "In every country we should hit their organizations, institutions, clubs and hospitals. The targets must be identified, carefully chosen and include their largest gatherings so that any strike should cause thousands of deaths."[62]

Terrorism in the twenty-first century is likely to involve weapons of mass destruction—chemical and biological agents and nuclear devices—and experts fear that the death toll will be staggering.

And as long as groups of people feel they have no other avenue to attain their political goals, whether legitimate or illegitimate, terrorism will remain a fact of life with which every person will have to contend. "We are all possible hostages to threats and intimidation, and potential victims of violent attacks," says political scientist Martin Miller.

Terror [has become] a factor in our everyday thinking and planning—we fear bombs and hijackings during plane flights, where we are so utterly vulner-

The twin towers of New York's World Trade Center (left) moments before their collapse. Firefighters (right) approach the wreckage of the Pentagon.

Timothy McVeigh and *The Turner Diaries*

On April 19, 1995, Timothy McVeigh, a disgruntled former U.S. Army gunner, detonated an enormous truck bomb outside the Murrah Federal Building in Oklahoma City, Oklahoma. The blast leveled half of the massive nine-story structure and killed 168 people. It was at that time, the most devastating act of terrorism perpetrated within the borders of the United States. McVeigh was convicted and executed for the crime. At his trial, federal prosecutors entered as evidence a copy of a novel called The Turner Diaries, *written by Andrew McDonald, a pen name of William Pierce, who had been a leader of the National Alliance, a rabidly pro-Nazi, white supremacist sect. During the testimony, it was revealed that the book was regarded as a "Bible" by American right-wing extremists and that McVeigh used it as a blueprint for his terrorist attack. In his study of religion-inspired terrorism,* Terror in the Mind of God, *sociologist Mark Juergensmeyer outlines the plot of* The Turner Diaries *and argues that it provides insight into the mind of McVeigh and other ultraconservative advocates and practitioners of political violence.*

"[*The Turner Diaries*] describes in chilling detail how the fictional hero blew up a federal building with a truckload of a 'little under 5,000 pounds' of ammonium nitrate fertilizer and fuel oil. Timothy McVeigh's own truck carried 4,400 pounds of the same mixture, packaged and transported exactly as described in the novel. According to Pierce's story, the purpose of the bombing was to launch an attack against the perceived evils of government and to arouse the fighting spirit of all 'free men.' According to Pierce, such efforts were necessary because the mindset of dictatorial secularism [godlessness] had been imposed on American society as the result of an elaborate conspiracy orchestrated by Jews and liberals hell-bent on depriving Christian society of its freedom and spiritual moorings. . . . Pierce [and other right-wing militants] believe that the great confrontation between freedom and a government-imposed slavery is close at hand and that their valiant . . . efforts can threaten the evil system and awaken the spirit of the freedom-loving masses."

able; we avoid certain neighborhoods or buildings. . . . In this sense, terrorism has succeeded to a large degree, not in attaining the specific objectives of any group or individual, but in making the threat of political violence a central concern in our lives. . . . Terrorism has become a permanent part of modern Western society . . . a highly active and very threatening form of violence with which we are only beginning to learn to cope.[63]

Notes

Introduction: Defining Terrorism

1. Quoted in David J. Whittaker, ed., *The Terrorism Reader*. London: Routledge, 2001, p. 6.
2. Quoted in Whittaker, *The Terrorism Reader*, p. 8.

Chapter One: Zealots, Assassins, and the Reign of Terror

3. Flavius Josephus, *The New Complete Works of Josephus*. Trans. William Whiston. Grand Rapids, MI: Kregel Publications, 1999, p. 747.
4. Quoted in Josephus, *The New Complete Works of Josephus*, p. 813.
5. Josephus, *The New Complete Works of Josephus*, p. 822.
6. Josephus, *The New Complete Works of Josephus*, p. 822.
7. Bruce Scott, "Roman Madness at Masada," 1998. www.foigm.org.
8. Anthony Campbell, *The Assassins of Alamut*. 1998. http://homepage.ntl-world.com.campbell/essays/publishing.html.
9. Marco Polo, *The Travels*. Trans. Ronald Latham. London: Penguin Books, 1958, p. 70.
10. Polo, *The Travels*, p. 70.
11. Maximilien Robespierre, "Speech on the Justification of the Use of Terror, February 5, 1774," in Paul Halsall, ed., Modern History Sourcebook. New York: Fordham University, 1998, p. 3.
12. Robespierre, "Speech on the Justification of the Use of Terror," in Halsall, Modern History Sourcebook, p. 3.
13. Edmund Burke, *Reflections on the Revolution in France*. Ed. Conor Cruise O'Brien. London: Penguin Books, 1968, p. 125.
14. Albert Parry, *Terrorism from Robespierre to Arafat*. New York: Vanguard Press, 1976, p. 40.

Chapter Two: Propaganda of the Bomb

15. Nikolai Morozov, "The Terrorist Struggle," in Walter Laqueur and Yonah Alexander, eds., *The Terrorism Reader*. New York: Meridian, 1987, p. 76.
16. Karl Heinzen, "Murder" in Laqueur and Alexander, *The Terrorism Reader*, pp. 53–59.
17. Walter Laqueur, *A History of Terrorism*. New Brunswick, NJ: Transaction Publishers, 2001, p. 36.
18. Quoted in Martin A. Miller, "The Intellectual Origins of Modern Terrorism in Europe," in Martha Crenshaw, ed., *Terrorism in Context*. University Park: Pennsylvania State University Press, 1995, p. 36.
19. Miller, "The Intellectual Origins of Modern Terrorism in Europe," in Crenshaw, *Terrorism in Context*, pp. 36–37.
20. Miller, "The Intellectual Origins of Modern Terrorism in Europe," in Crenshaw, *Terrorism in Context*, p. 38.
21. Quoted in Parry, *Terrorism from Robespierre to Arafat*, p. 87.
22. Borijove Jevtic, "28 June, 1914: The Assassination of Archduke Franz Ferdinand," *World War I Document Archive*, Brigham Young University, 2001. www.lib.byu.edu/~rdh/wwi/1914/ferd dead.html.
23. Quoted in Jevtic, "28 June, 1914: The Assassination of Archduke Franz Ferdinand."

24. Laqueur, *A History of Terrorism*, p. 82.

Chapter Three: Anticolonial Terrorism

25. Quoted in Bruce Hoffman, *Inside Terrorism*. New York: Columbia University Press, 1998, p. 47.
26. Hoffman, *Inside Terrorism*, p. 48.
27. Quoted in Ian S. Lustick, "Terrorism in the Arab-Israeli Conflict: Targets and Audiences," in Crenshaw, *Terrorism in Context*, p. 522.
28. Hoffman, *Inside Terrorism*, p. 50.
29. Quoted in Hoffman, *Inside Terrorism*, p. 53.
30. Quoted in Hoffman, *Inside Terrorism*, p. 56.
31. Quoted in Hoffman, *Inside Terrorism*, p. 61.
32. Robert Kumamoto, *International Terrorism and American Foreign Relations 1945–1976*. Boston: Northeastern University Press, 1999, pp. 77–78.
33. Martha Crenshaw, "The Effectiveness of Terrorism in the Algerian War," in Crenshaw, *Terrorism in Context*, pp. 475–82.

Chapter Four: Terrorism and the Left

34. Quoted in Parry, *Terrorism from Robespierre to Arafat*, p. 395.
35. Whittaker, *The Terrorism Reader*, p. 194.
36. Parry, *Terrorism from Robespierre to Arafat*, p. 400.
37. Whittaker, *The Terrorism Reader*, p. 196.
38. Quoted in Ehud Sprinzak, "The Psychological Formation of Extreme Left Terrorism in a Democracy: The Case of the Weathermen," in Walter Reich, ed., *Origins of Terrorism*. Washington, DC: Woodrow Wilson Center Press, 1998, pp. 65–67.
39. Quoted in Parry, *Terrorism from Robespierre to Arafat*, p. 335.
40. Sprinzak, "The Psychological Formation of Extreme Left Terrorism in a Democracy," in Reich, *Origins of Terrorism*, p. 78.

41. Quoted in Whittaker, *The Terrorism Reader*, p. 196.
42. Paul Furlong, "Political Terrorism in Italy: Responses, Reaction, and Immobilism," in Whittaker, *The Terrorism Reader*, pp. 206–207.
43. Furlong, "Political Terrorism in Italy," in Whittaker, *The Terrorism Reader*, p. 208.
44. Parry, *Terrorism from Robespierre to Arafat*, p. 278.

Chapter Five: Separatist Terrorism

45. Laqueur, *A History of Terrorism*, p. 190.
46. Quoted in Whittaker, *The Terrorism Reader*, p. 182.
47. *Belfast Telegraph*, "The Troubles," 1997. www.belfasttelegraph.co.uk/niguide/troubles.html.
48. *Belfast Telegraph*, "The Troubles."
49. Goldie Shabad and F.J.L. Ramos, "Political Violence in a Democratic State: Basque Terrorism in Spain," in Crenshaw, *Terrorism in Context*, p. 419.
50. Parry, *Terrorism from Robespierre to Arafat*, p. 410.
51. Jose A. Trevino, "Spain's Internal Security: The Basque Autonomous Police Force," in Whittaker, *The Terrorism Reader*, p. 134.
52. Walter Laqueur, *The New Terrorism*. New York: Oxford University Press, 1999, pp. 34–36.

Chapter Six: Holy War

53. Parry, *Terrorism from Robespierre to Arafat*, p. 449.
54. BBC News World Service, "Black September: Tough Negotiations." London: British Broadcasting Corporation, 2001. http://news.bbc.co.uk/english/in_dep… confidential/newsid_10890000/1089694/stm.
55. Hoffman, *Inside Terrorism*, p. 72.
56. Hoffman, *Inside Terrorism*, p. 73.

57. Quoted in Hoffman, *Inside Terrorism*, p. 95.

58. Israel Information Service, "Hizballah IDF." Jerusalem: Information Division Israel Foreign Ministry, 1994. www.alma shriq.hiof.no/lebanon/300/32...324.2/hiz ballah/hizballah-ifm-9401.html.

59. Quoted in Martin Kramer, "The Moral Logic of Hizballah," in Reich, *Origins of Terrorism*, pp. 144–45.

60. Laqueur, *The New Terrorism*, p. 139.

61. Quoted in Mark Juergensmeyer, *Terror in the Mind of God*. Berkeley: University of California Press, 2000, p. 153.

62. Quoted in Hamza Hendawi, "Terror Manual Lists Top Targets for Destruction," *Palm Beach Post*, February 2, 2002, p. 6A.

63. Miller, "The Intellectual Origins of Modern Terrorism in Europe," p. 62.

For Further Reading

Books

Hal Marcovitz, *Terrorism*. Philadelphia, PA: Chelsea House, 2001. This book contains a detailed account of several terrorist incidents, especially the murder of Israeli athletes at the 1972 Munich Olympics by Arab terrorists and the kidnapping of newspaper heiress Patty Hearst by the Symbionese Liberation Army in 1974. However, it does not offer much in the way of analysis, nor does it put the events it describes in historical context. The description is dramatic and the book is easy to read.

Jonathan R. White, *Terrorism: An Introduction*. Belmont, CA: Wadsworth, 1998. The author starts with an analysis of the different motivations for terrorism and proceeds to a historical account of terrorist activity, broken down into geographical region. The approach enables him to stress the similarities and differences between various terrorist organizations.

Internet Sources

ICT: The Interdisciplinary Center, (www.ict. org.il/home.cfm). The ICT is an Israeli counterterrorism think tank and information clearing-house. Its site contains links to an impressive number of articles on terrorism, with a focus on terrorist groups that have played a role in the history of the Middle East.

The Terrorism Research Center (www.terror ism.com). The Terrorism Research Center is a private group specializing in the study of terrorism and methods of prevention and response. Its site contains a brief history of the subject and links to other valuable sources of information.

Terrorist and Insurgent Organizations, (www.au.af.mil/au/bibs/tergps/tg98tc. htm). The Air University Library at Maxwell Air Force Base in Alabama maintains this site, which includes links to historical profiles of the major terrorist groups.

U.S. Department of State: Counterterrorism Office (www.state.gov/s/ct). This site is a gateway to a vast amount of information on terrorism, including the history of active terrorist groups, compiled by various agencies of the U.S. government.

WWW-VL History Central Catalogue, (www.ukans.edu/history/VL). This site, maintained by the University of Kansas, provides access to documents and analyses pertaining to countries whose history has been affected by terrorism. Follow the comprehensive index to find relevant information.

Works Consulted

Books

Edmund Burke, *Reflections on the Revolution in France*. Ed. Conor Cruise O'Brien. London: Penguin Books, 1968. Burke was a conservative British politician and political theorist who urged the leaders of the French Revolution to abandon their more radical goals, stop the violence, and restore the monarchy.

Martha Crenshaw, ed., *Terrorism in Context*. University Park, PA: Pennsylvania State University Press, 1995. This book is a collection of scholarly essays dealing with various aspects of modern terrorism. Part I, which covers terrorism in 19th century Europe and Russia, is especially informative.

Philip S. Foner, ed., *The Black Panthers Speak*. Cambridge, MA: Da Capo Press, 1995. Foner has collected a broad selection of writings by various members of the Black Panther Party and their supporters. The book provides insight into how a racial minority came to view themselves as a captive colony within the United States and how their anti-colonialist ideology led them to believe that terrorism was a valid response to their predicament.

Paul Halsall, ed., *Modern History Sourcebook*. New York: Fordham University, 1998. A collection of historical documents arranged by era and geography. The material is presented in English translations.

Bruce Hoffman, *Inside Terrorism*. New York: Columbia University Press, 1998. Hoffman is a consultant on counterterrorism to the governments of the United States and other countries. His book is a clear exposition of the evolution of modern terrorism in terms of tactics and objectives.

Flavius Josephus, *The New Complete Works of Josephus*. Trans. William Whiston. Grand Rapids, MI: Kregel Publications, 1999. Josephus provides a comprehensive view of the turmoil caused by the Jewish resistance to the Roman occupation of Palestine in the first century A.D. The translation is somewhat stilted but nonetheless readable. Josephus was a participant in the events he describes, and subsequent scholars claim he was not always unbiased.

Mark Juergensmeyer, *Terror in the Mind of God*. Berkeley: The University of California Press, 2000. The author, a sociologist, contends that religion-inspired terrorists are especially dangerous because they believe their violence is helping to bring about a divinely ordained plan for humankind and is thus justified by God. The book is intended for a nonscholarly audience, and Juergensmeyer makes his case clearly and compellingly.

Robert Kumamoto, *International Terrorism and American Foreign Relations 1945–1976*. Boston: Northeastern University Press, 1999. Kumamoto looks at the history of terrorism between the years 1945 and 1976 from the viewpoint of how political violence around the world influenced American foreign policy decisions. In the case of Israel and

Algeria, that influence, he concludes, was substantial.

Walter Laqueur and Yonah Alexander, eds, *The Terrorism Reader*. New York: Meridian books, 1987. Laqueur and Alexander have assembled a series of excerpts from books and articles covering the entire history of terrorism from ancient times to the late 20th century. Each section of the book is introduced by a helpful background essay.

———, *The New Terrorism*. New York: Oxford University Press, 1999. In this book, Laqueur examines the forms that terrorism will take in the twenty-first century. He also makes numerous references to the history of earlier terrorism and makes the case that the phenomenon is becoming potentially more deadly as technological advances make weapons of mass destruction available to small groups of political extremists.

Walter Laqueur and Yonah Alexander, eds., *The Terrorism Reader*. New York: Meridian, 1987.

Albert Parry, *Terrorism from Robespierre to Arafat*. New York: Vanguard Press, 1976. Parry was forced to flee Russia during the Communist Revolution. His experiences made him an unswerving foe of terrorism in all its forms. This comprehensive history is factually accurate but one-sided in its interpretation of the events and people it discusses.

Marco Polo, *The Travels*. Trans. Ronald Latham. London: Penguin Books, 1958. Polo visited the Assassin stronghold of Alamut in the year 1271, shortly before it was overrun by the Mongols. He recorded stories told to him by the successors of the organization's founder.

Walter Reich, ed., *Origins of Terrorism*. Washington, DC: Woodrow Wilson Center Press, 1998. Reich provides a useful introduction to the history of terrorism in this collection of scholarly essays.

John Richard Thackrah, *Encyclopedia of Terrorism and Political Violence*. London: Routledge & Kegan Paul, 1987. This concise reference book is useful but sometimes sacrifices coherence in the interest of brevity. It is written from a counterterrorism perspective that treats the phenomenon largely as a law enforcement problem.

David J. Whittaker, ed., *The Terrorism Reader*. London: Routledge, 2001. A collection of writings from the works of a number of contemporary students of terrorism. The focus is on the causes of terrorist violence in various regions of the world.

Periodicals

Hamza Hendawi, "Terror Manual Lists Top Targets for Destruction," *Palm Beach Post*, February 2, 2002.

Parama Roy, "Discovering India, Imagining Thuggee," *Yale Journal of Criticism*, 1998.

Internet Sources

Algerian National Liberation Front, "Proclamation of the Algerian National Liberation Front," 1954. http://historicaltextarchive.com/sections.php?op=viewarticle&artid=10. The proclamation couches the goals of the National Liberation Front in diplomatic language, masking the intensity of terrorist violence of which they were capable.

BBC News World Service, "Black September: Tough Negotiations." London: British Broadcasting Corporation, 2001. http://news.bbc.co.uk/english/in_dep…confidential/newsid_10890000/1089694

/stm. This retrospective story details the tense negotiations between the British government and Black September over the release of airplane hjacker Leila Khaled and the animosity the British decision to release her created between the governments of Britain, Israel, and the United States.

Belfast Telegraph, "The Troubles," 1997. www.belfasttelegraph.co.uk/niguide/ troubles.html. This article is part of a series of background pieces on terrorism in Northern Ireland prepared by the staff of the *Belfast Telegraph.* The series is a concise introduction to the problems and history of the violence that has plagued Northern Ireland since the late 1960s.

Anthony Campbell, *The Assassins of Alamut.* 1998. http://homepage. ntlworld.com. campbell/essays/publishing.html. Although self-published on the Internet, this book-length account of the Assassins is scholarly, balanced, and readable. The author claims he chose this mode of publication to reach a wider readership.

Israel Information Service, "Hizballah IDF." Jerusalem: Information Division Israel Foreign Ministry, 1994. www.almashriq.hiof.no/lebanon/300/ 32…324.2/hizballah/hizballah-ifm-9401.html. This press release from the Israeli government provides a brief background on the Hizballah terrorism.

Borijove Jevtic, "28 June, 1914: The Assassination of Archduke Franz Ferdinand," *World War I Document Archive,* Brigham Young University, 2001. www.lib.byu.edu/~rdh/wwi/1914/ ferddead.html. A short (two-page) account of the assassination of Archduke Franz Ferdinand, the terrorist event that helped to precipitate the First World War. Jevtic was a member of the assassination squad.

Bruce Scott, "Roman Madness at Masada," 1998. www.foigm.org. A concise account of the fall of Masada; relies heavily on Josephus's account in *The Jewish War.*

Leon Trotsky, *Why Marxists Oppose Individual Terrorism.* 1909. www.marx ists.org/archive/trotsky/works/ 1090.htm. Trotsky was the most thoughtful and scholarly of the Russian revolutionaries. His motive in writing this short work was to counter the various anarchist movements that were vying with the Communist Party for support among the workers and peasantry in the early twentieth century. The work is polemical in the sense that it tries to persuade the reader to agree with its author's point of view, but it is also a clear statement of the Marxist position on a topic that was hotly debated at the time.

Index

Picture Credits

Cover: Wire Image
© AFP/CORBIS, 68
Archivoiconografico, S.A./CORBIS, 23
© Bettmann/CORBIS, 15, 18, 24, 26, 28, 34, 35, 40, 43, 48, 54, 57, 58, 64, 65, 67, 72, 74, 76
Bibliotheque National/Bridgemann Art Library, 19
Bridgeman Art Library, 14

Chris Jouan, 22, 39
© CORBIS, 30, 31, 44
Hulton Archive, 36, 51 (both), 62
Hulton-Deutsch Collection/CORBIS, 41, 47, 49, 71
© Nathan Benn/CORBIS, 9, 69, 77, 79, 80 (both)
© Reuters New Media/CORBIS, 9, 69, 77, 79, 80 (both)

About the Author

Robert Taylor has written on science, technology, history, politics, law, philosophy, medicine, and contemporary culture. He lives in West Palm Beach, Florida.

DATE DUE

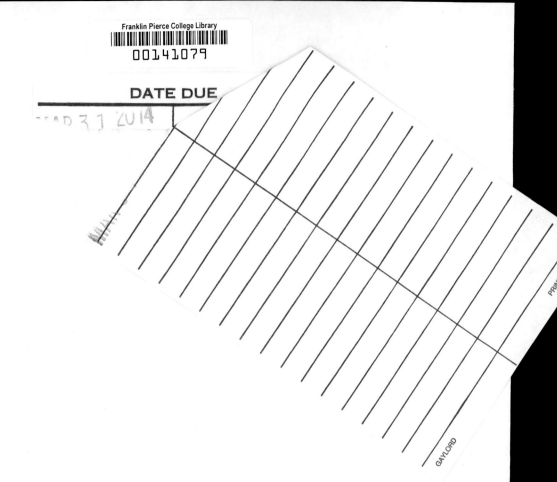

GAYLORD

PRINT